James J. Owen, Frederick P Evans

Psychography;

Marvelous manifestations of psychic power given through the mediumship of Fred

P. Evans

James J. Owen, Frederick P Evans

Psychography;
Marvelous manifestations of psychic power given through the mediumship of Fred P. Evans

ISBN/EAN: 9783337815233

Printed in Europe, USA, Canada, Australia, Japan

Cover: Foto ©ninafisch / pixelio.de

More available books at **www.hansebooks.com**

PSYCHOGRAPHY

MARVELOUS MANIFESTATIONS

OF

PSYCHIC POWER

GIVEN THROUGH THE MEDIUMSHIP OF

FRED P. EVANS

KNOWN AS

THE "INDEPENDENT SLATE-WRITER"

BY J. J. OWEN

Late Editor of the "GOLDEN GATE," and Author of "OUR SUNDAY TALKS,
"SPIRITUAL FRAGMENTS," Etc.

THE HICKS-JUDD CO.
PRINTERS, BOOKBINDERS AND PUBLISHERS
23 FIRST STREET, SAN FRANCISCO

✜

TO ALL SOULS SEEKING FOR TRUTH,
OR A KNOWLEDGE OF LIFE
BEYOND THE GRAVE,
THIS VOLUME
IS RESPECTFULLY DEDICATED

✜

64859

TABLE OF CONTENTS.

	PAGE.
Preface	7
Introductory	9
Biographical Sketch	19
Fred Evans in San Jose	28
Psychomo Lodge	35
Extraordinary Phenomena	39
A Slate of Many Languages	41
Spirit Art	52
Seance with Professor A. R. Wallace	54
Through Southern California	61
Fred Evans at Los Angeles	70
Mr. Ausbach's "Exposé"	74
Challenge Accepted	76
The Spirit World	77
At the Opera House	80
Our Psychic in Santa Barbara	82
Mr. and Mrs. Evans in Stockton	87
A *Mail* Skeptic Disarmed	89
Stanley St. Clair	93
Tests by Proxy	98
Spirit Camelia	100
An Interesting Experiment	105
Spirit John Gray	108
Remarkable Experience	111
Spirit Josephine	113
St. Clair's Picture of Shakespeare	118
A Spirit Indian Maiden	121
Mr. and Mrs. Evans' Trip to Australia	127
Before the Psychological Society of Brisbane	136
Color Tests and Portrait Drawing	139
Painful Accident	142
Experiments in Other Phases	144
Passing Matter Through Matter	147
Physical Manifestations	150
A Seance with Fred Evans	155
Mr. Evans' Departure from Brisbane	159
What Mr. Somerville Says	163
Fred Evans in Melbourne	165
Public Demonstration of Psychography at Horticultural Hall, Melbourne	172
A Sealed Letter Answered	178
Departure from Melbourne	179
What a Brother of Senator Stanford Says	181
Mr. Fred Evans in Sydney	182

TABLE OF CONTENTS.

	PAGE.
He Confounds the Jugglers	184
Letter from Jenny Wren	186
Strong Endorsement	189
Tests not in the Dark	191
I Attend a Seance	192
Letter from Charles P. Cocks	193
Words Spoken at a Funeral	198
Skepticism and Its Effects	200
A Question of Proof	203
How the Writing Is Done	206
Conclusion	211

TABLE OF ILLUSTRATIONS.

	PAGE.
First Slate Given Before a Public Audience	26
Professor Robert Hare	34
Slate of Twelve Languages	42
Slate Obtained at a Select Seance	50
D. D. Home	53
John Pierpont	58
Dr. Benjamin Rush	67
Mrs. Breed	75
Our Spirit Artist	96
Spirit Camelia	101
Slate for Mr. Whitlock	105
John Gray	109
Josephine	115
St. Clair's Shakespeare	119
Indian Maiden	122
Professor Denton	125
Slate Produced Before the Brisbane Psychological Society	137
Passing Matter Through Matter	148
Brass Collar	151
Portrait for Editor of *Psychic Notes*	154
Fac-Simile of Direct Spirit Writing in Colors	173
How the Writing Is Done	209

Preface.

MOST of the experiments mentioned in this volume were made either in the presence of the author, and under the most crucial test conditions, or in the presence of others in whom the writer has the utmost confidence. These experiments are none the less valuable now that a few years have elapsed since their occurrence. The fact is that the multiplicity of other duties devolving upon the author has prevented the devotion of the necessary time to the preparation of this book, until a short time prior to its publication. Some of the best results given herein, however, have been produced since the commencement of the pleasant task of preparing the copy for the printer—showing that the mediumistic powers of Fred Evans have lost none of their vigor or reliability. We may add that we have written in the past no word of endorsement of this gifted psychic that we would wish to recall. To us the writing comes with the same readiness and completeness now as ever. In conferring with Mr. Evans' guide a few days prior to this writing, to consult with him concerning the arrangement and plan of this volume, Spirit John Gray came to us with a hearty " God bless you, my dear Mr. Owen," and proceeded to fill nine slates full of writing directly under our own hands. He said, "I am more than pleased to see that you have used a little persuasion to have Fred permit you to proceed at once with his book, for I wish to see it published and ready for the public as soon as possible." He then named the pages and volumes of the *Golden Gate*, wherein we would find matter suitable for the book, and made valuable suggestions concerning the arrangements of the cuts, etc. He subsequently, at our request, wrote a fine article explanatory of the methods whereby the writing is done upon the slates by psychic power. This article appears in full under the heading, " How the Writing Is Done," and is the best exposition of that subject we have yet seen. To us this work is one of real pleasure, as we trust its perusal will be to all searchers after the truth.

Respectfully,

THE AUTHOR.

Introductory.

THE grave is no longer voiceless. It speaks to us with myriad tongues and in many ways. The marvelous manifestations of occult power that have occurred at rare intervals along the line of human history, and that were generally regarded as miraculous interpositions of Divine Providence, have come to be almost as common as human life. To longer doubt the phenomena of spirit intercourse, or regard its varied manifestations as tricks of jugglery, is to indicate that the doubter has been left behind in the march of events and is groping amid the shadows of the past.

To millions of homes the fact of communion with the so-called dead is as familiar as intercourse with the living on the mortal plane. They have their oracles, or psychics, in mothers, wives, and often in little children, and so perfect has the way of communication become that communion by entrancement, by clairvoyance, by clairaudience, by the spirit rap, and often in other ways, is common and instantaneous, without resort to the circle or to any special condition.

And thus have the dark clouds of ages of theological error been swept away, and the gloom and night of the grave been illumined by the positive sunlight of the new truth that has dawned upon the world. We now lay away our idols, not to sleep in the grave until some far-away resurrection of the physical body shall call them forth to endless happiness or woe, but we simply consign "dust to dust," knowing that the spirit, clad in the habiliments of immortal youth, still lives to comfort the mourner with the sweet thought that they are not dead.

How little do we really know of the nature of spirit. We live in a world of mysteries—the mystery of being, of birth, growth, death—the mystery of hidden forces and laws—some of which, by familiarity therewith, have ceased to make us wonder, but which are none the less mysteries.

What do we know of the occult power that projected man upon this whirling ball of earth, and made him a sentient, conscious being, with marvelous faculties and powers? What do we know of plant life and growth, of electricity, of the laws of gravitation, of combustion, of the principles of attraction and cohesion, of many other properties of matter? How does the rose extract its colors and perfume from the earth and air? What gives the bee the instinct of a coming time when the earth will be barren of its food supply?

And thus we might go on questioning, almost indefinitely, concerning a vast array of nature's manifestations with which, in a certain sense, we are familiar, but with the inner meanings and principles of which we know little or nothing.

Placed as we are in the midst of mysteries most wonderful and profound, why should intelligent man question the possibility of spirit return and communion, which is really no more mysterious than the intelligent communion of mortals? The moving of ponderous bodies by an intelligent, invisible power, is no more mysterious than many other manifestations of the forces with which we are more familiar.

Notwithstanding the logic of all the mystery with which nature abounds, there are multitudes of intelligent people who ignore and deny all of the essential facts upon which Spiritualists base their claims concerning a future existence. Some scientists even treat the subject with ridicule, and affect a superiority of wisdom concerning the same, which is as amazing as it is pitiful. But "the world moves" nevertheless. The truth is certain to come uppermost at last.

The phenomenalism of Spiritualism will soon, as other newly discovered principles and forces in nature have done in the past, cease to excite especial wonder. The spirit rap; the temporary domination of natural law by a higher but none the less natural law; the trance, clairvoyance, clairaudience, psychography, psychometry; the exercise of all the many and varied gifts of the spirit, and last, but by no means least, the wonderful manifestation of the psychic form—all these, and more, will soon be as familiar to mankind as human life itself. The knowledge of these facts is spreading with marvelous rapidity throughout the world.

When Professor Zöllner, in his experiments, demonstrated the power of the spirit scientist to disintegrate matter and again reunite the particles of the same—that is, to pass matter through matter without any apparent derangement of the particles thereof—he gave to the thoughtful mind a suggestive hint of the true relation of spirit to the material universe.

In our own experiments with psychic force, we have, time and again, verified the great German Professor's conclusions, in demonstrating to our entire satisfaction the possibility of projecting matter through matter by spirit power. Similar experiments have been made and like conclusions reached by all careful students in this realm of occult forces, the summing up of which teaches us, beyond questioning, the stupendous fact that matter is servant of the spirit—that it is the evanescent and unreal, while spirit is the only truly potent and substantial thing in the universe.

After all, what is spirit but a higher and superior form of matter? Where can we draw the dividing line? Certainly not at the point of invisibility, for there are worlds of matter all around us that no eye can see. The air, the perfume of the rose, the imponderable ether, even, is a rarefied form of matter. In fact we can conceive of nothing that is not matter. We call its finer forms spirit, to distinguish them from the coarser, but it is matter all the same. In the nature of things, the finer and superior must dominate the coarser. All worlds and systems of worlds swing through the mighty spaces of the skies in perfect obedience to a Something which is infinitely more potent than they.

To the most superficial thinker the ponderability of matter is merely conditional, and these conditions are continually changing. The most obdurate metals may be consumed by acids or dissipated by heat. The diamond itself, the hardest of all known substances, is but a crystal of carbon, that may be scattered as with a breath. There is no form of matter that may not be changed to other forms by a power behind it greater than itself, which is simply the higher, or spiritual, varying its modes of expression.

The lesson of these facts should teach man that he is something more than a clod—that there is that within him greater than he seems—a something of which his physical body is but the expression. If there were no positive evidence of man's spiritual existence after he has cast aside the earthly form, it would seem that the inference of such an existence, drawn from the varied phenomena of life, would be irresistible.

Why do we hope for that which it would be absolutely and forever impossible to attain? Can the materialist answer? Is it reasonable to suppose that nature would stand and make faces at herself? Is there anything in all her teachings that warrants the conclusion that she is petulant, or childish, or false? We think not. And this conclusion becomes more and more irresistible as we delve deeper and deeper in the mine of spiritual knowledge.

Professors Alfred R. Wallace, Crookes, Varley, Zöllner, Hellenbach, Flammarian, Hare, and other eminent scientists, devoted years to the investigation of spirit phenomena, and became thoroughly convinced that they were the incontrovertible evidences of independent spirit existence. Other scientists, to which may be added the Harvard professors, and a vast array of superficial thinkers of all classes, who never gave the subject more than a passing thought—never sat in a seance, or, if they did, it was for the purpose, if possible, of detecting a supposed trick—denounce all the manifestations of psychic power as the works of jugglery, or attribute them to unconscious cerebration, involuntary muscular action, or some half dozen other six-syllabled and nonsensical reasons.

Now, we respectfully ask, Which of the two classes is better entitled to belief? Is the man who has demonstrated a proposition or principle to his satisfaction, and knows it to be true, to be thrust aside and his opinions ridiculed by one who simply does not know what he is talking about? Will the honest skeptic accept the *ipse dixit* of the latter? And yet that is seemingly what many are doing. They accept explanations for natural phenomena that, when submitted to the crucible of the most ordinary reason, are dispelled into vapor.

But why is it that people—especially religious people—should be so hostile to the demonstrated facts of spirit existence? They claim to believe in it as a matter of faith, why should they be averse to the truth—to having the fact placed beyond question of doubt? Even the materialist and skeptic should be ready to hail with joy a truth of such stupendous moment; at least they should listen impartially to the evidence, and not prejudge the case.

Nature is full of surprises to whoever has the courage to follow her hidden ways and the skill to discover her secrets. Reasoning man should not shrink from the investigation of whatever relates to his present or future welfare. There is nothing that belongs to his life that he has not a right to know—nothing in nature that does not belong to him—the good to be appropriated to his own use and happiness; the evil or hurtful to be placed under his feet.

This would seem to be the true course to pursue with regard to all things in earth or the heavens above—to all sources of human knowledge.

The following is a list of some eminent persons who, after

personal investigation, have satisfied themselves of the reality of some of the phenomena generally known as Psychical or Spiritualistic.

SCIENCE.—The Earl of Crawford and Balcarres, F. R. S., President R. A. S.; W. Crookes, Fellow and Gold Medalist of the Royal Society; C. Varley, F. R. S., C. E.; A. R. Wallace, the eminent Naturalist; W. F. Barrett, F. R. S. E., Professor of Physics in the Royal College of Science, Dublin; Dr. Lockhart Robertson; *Dr. J. Elliotson, F. R. S., sometime President of the Royal Medical and Chirurgical Society of London; *Professor de Morgan, sometime President of the Mathematical Society of London; *Dr. William Gregory, F. R. S. E., sometime Professor of Chemistry in the University of Edinburgh; *Dr. Ashburner; *Mr. Rutter; *Dr. Herbert Mayo, F. R. S., etc., etc.

*Professor F. Zöllner, of Leipzig, author of "Transcendental Physics," etc.; Professors G. T. Fechner, Scheibner, and J. H. Fichte, of Leipzig; Professor W. E. Weber, of Göttingen; Professor Hoffman, of Würzburg; *Professor Perty, of Berne; Professors Wagner and *Butlerof, of Petersburg; *Professors Hare and Mapes, of U. S. A.; Dr. Robert Friese, of Breslau; M. Camille Flammarian, Astronomer, etc., etc.

LITERATURE.—The Earl of Dunraven; T. A. Trollope; S. C. Hall; Gerald Massey; Sir R. Burton; *Professor Cassal, LL. D.; *Lord Brougham; *Lord Lytton; *Lord Lyndhurst; *Archbishop Whately; *Dr. R. Chambers, F. R. S. E.; *W. M. Thackeray; *Nassau Senior; *George Thompson; *W. Howitt; *Sergeant Cox; *Mrs. Browning; Hon. Roden Noel, etc., etc.

Bishop Clarke, Rhode Island, U. S. A.; Darius Lyman, U. S. A.; Professor W. Denton; Professor Alex. Wilder; Professor Hiram Corson; Professor George Bush; and twenty four Judges and ex-Judges of the United States Courts; *Victor Hugo; Baron and Baroness Von Vay; *W. Lloyd Garrison, U. S. A.; *Hon. R. Dale Owen, U. S. A.; *Hon. J. W. Edmonds, U. S. A.; *Epes Sargent; *Baron du Potet; *Count A. de Gasparin; *Baron L. de Guldenstübbe, etc., etc.

SOCIAL POSITION.—H. I. H. Nicholas, Duke of Leuchtenberg; H. R. H. the Prince of Solms; H. S. H. Prince Albrecht of Solms; *H. S. H. Prince Emile of Sayn-Wittgenstein; Hon. Alexander Aksakof, Imperial Councilor of Russia; the Countess of Caithness and Duchesse de Pomar; the Hon. J. L. O'Sullivan, sometime Minister of U. S. A. at the Court of Lisbon; M. Favre-Clavairoz, late Consul-General of France at Trieste; the late Emperors of *Russia and *France; Presidents *Thiers and *Lincoln, etc., etc.

N. B. An asterisk is prefixed to those who have exchanged belief for knowledge.

Psychography, or writing by spirit power, is not new to the world, if we may believe the sacred writings of the ancients. When the Spirit inscribed upon tables of stone, for Moses, in the mountains of Sinai, those marvelous lessons of wisdom and law known as the Ten Commandments, what was it but a higher form of independent writing? And again, when the carousing hosts of Belshazzar paused in their mad revelry, and, paralyzed with fear, gazed upon the spirit hand writing upon the wall those prophetic words, "*Mene, mene, tekel upharsin*" (This day shall thy kingdom be taken from thee), what grander illustration of psychography was ever presented to the world?

In the preparation of this book, devoted as it will be mainly to the psychographic powers of Fred P. Evans, we hope to preserve a record of some most remarkable incidents that cannot but prove valuable to investigators in psychic phenomena.

The writer first became acquainted with Fred Evans, the gifted psychographist, in the summer of 1885. We were editing the *Golden Gate* at that time, a paper "devoted to practical reform, the uplifting of humanity in this life, and a search for the evidences of life beyond." Mr. Evans (a biographical sketch of whose life is herein given) had then but recently entered the field of public work as an independent slate-writer.

We were well informed on the subject of psychography, as witnessed in the presence of Mrs. Hollis, so graphically described by her able biographer, Dr. Wolff, and of William Eglinton, of England, as given in his own elegant work. We also had had much personal experience with that, at one time, excellent slate-writer, Mrs. Clara S. Reid, and also with Mrs. C. M. Stowe, and had witnessed the phenomenon in the presence of several others, all more or less satisfactory.

With all of these psychics it was necessary to hold the slate under a table, and out of sight of the sitter, a condition never entirely satisfactory to the skeptic. Fred Evans was able to procure the writing in the open light of day, without contact of hands, by simply placing the slates upon a table, or upon the floor, within a few feet of the psychic. In this way we have received as many as fourteen slates at one sitting, written full upon the under side, the message continuing from one slate to another, all upon matters of much interest to us, and all written in a few minutes' time.

And here is a phase of this phenomenon of amazing interest to all searchers into the realm of the occult. While one can often hear the pencil tip moving over the under surface of the slate, the writing is quite as often, with Mr. Evans especially, apparently thrown or impressed upon the slate, vastly more rapidly than it could possibly be written by mortal hand.

We recall one instance where some twelve hundred words were finely written over the surfaces of two large slates in what seemed to us an incredibly short space of time. We immediately, without any previous arrangement with, or intimation to, the medium, asked John Gray, his psychographic control, if he could name the number of words upon each slate. Instantly the correct figures were given, as we afterwards ascertained by careful count.

It is this open-handed way of writing that, in a large measure, has made Fred Evans pre-eminent among psychics for this phase, and given to him a world-wide reputation.

But all do not receive the positive demonstration of spirit power alike. Much depends upon the sitter. With some it is almost impossible to procure the writing at all, and then there may probably be defects in the message received—discrepancies in names or dates—which will not be satisfying to either medium or sitter. With others, and by far the larger number, the writing comes promptly, often giving names, dates, and other evidences of genuineness that sweep away all barriers of doubt and unbelief.

The writer, who has had hundreds of experimental seances with this psychic, the result of many of which will be given in the body of this work, is peculiarly fortunate in this respect. For him the writing comes always and readily, without the touch of the psychic's hands to the slates, and anywhere within the radius of eight or ten feet of his person. We have often, in his presence, sent out our thoughts to the spirit we would like to communicate with, and straightway the message would appear under our hands, and frequently in writing identical with that of the mortal whose spirit we had evoked, and sometimes accompanied by messages from spirits who were not in our thought at the time, thus disproving any supposition of mind-reading. Such proofs of spirit power or identity it would be unwise to deny.

Mr. Evans possesses other phases of psychic power; but he has wisely confined himself, in his public work, mainly to the one in which he felt he could produce the most satisfactory results.

The main source of Fred Evans' power is the intelligent entity, invisible to mortal eyes, that ever attends him, and who gives his name as John Gray, or, as his many friends familiarly call him, Johnny Gray. It is well known that spirits engaged in public work sometimes forsake their mediums for others, through whom they can accomplish better results. Such was the case with John Gray, who accompanied the psychic with whom Mr. Evans first sat for development, being assured by this spirit that he (Evans) possessed remarkable powers for the slate-writing phase. John Gray found Fred the better psychic of the two, and, forsaking the old instrument, took to the new, and has been with him from the time of his development to the present time, a period at this writing of nearly eight years.

Mr. Evans has in his band another spirit named Stanley St. Clair, an artist who came to him during the writer's experimental work with this psychic. It is this spirit who makes all the off-hand sketches of persons and scenes that frequently appear upon the slates. This spirit gave us a sketch of his life which will appear further on.

On one occasion St. Clair sketched for us a quaint scene of an old German town, where he said he had formerly pursued the study of his art. It was a characteristic sketch, and showed much ingenuity. The small windows and red roof tiles were true to nature, and could only have been sketched by one familiar with German scenery, which Mr. Evans certainly was not.

The frequent writing in colors that appears upon the slates, and that apparently without the use of colored crayons, is a most mysterious phase of this phenomenon. We have obtained as many as thirty-three shades of colors on a single slate. This color writing, we are aware, is not peculiar to Mr. Evans' guides alone, but we have never known a psychographist through whom the colors came in such great variety and profusion.

How is this colored writing done? John Gray explains that he extracts the colors from the elements, by spirit chemistry—often from flowers, or colored materials in proximity with the psychic. A lady medium for this phase informs us that the carpet in the room where she holds her seances had been despoiled of most of its colors by the spirits!

Wishing to ascertain if Spirit John Gray's powers for producing color writing were the same as when we had last tested him for that phase, some two years before, we called at the residence of Mr. Evans on Tuesday evening, December 27, 1892, when, under the usual crucial conditions, a personal message was written to the author, signed by eleven of his friends in spirit life, and all in different shades of color—some of them most delicate and exquisite. There were in all twelve shades of color upon the slate. The writing was produced under our own hands, no mortal hand touching the slate except those of the writer and his wife. The names and message are all of a personal character, but its chief merit to investigators is in the variety of colors, and the fact that they are written over a cross first placed upon the slate with a common slate pencil, to show that there was no false bottom to, or chemical preparation of, the slate, as jugglers or skeptics are disposed to assert.

We may add that upon several of the slates given in this volume there was some colored writing, or illustrations, which we have printed uniformly in black.

With this introduction we will pass on to other, and perhaps more interesting matter.

BIOGRAPHICAL SKETCH.

MR. FRED P. EVANS was born in Liverpool, England, June 9, 1862. He is rather under medium stature, is youthful in appearance, with pleasant features, and of fine health and physique. He was subject, in early life, to strange psychical experiences which indicated his mediumistic nature, but concerning which he then had no knowledge.

Fred came of a truly noble ancestry. One of his great-grandfathers was no less a personage than that grand humanitarian and reformer, Robert Owen. His great-grandmother, Catherine Owen, was a daughter of Hugh Hughes. His grandfather was Hugh Evans, and his grandmother's maiden name was Jane Owen, a granddaughter of Robert Owen. His grandparents were of Welsh nationality, his grandmother being first cousin to Lord Dinorben, of Cimal Hall, Denbigshire. His grandfather, Hugh Evans, was a prominent member of the old Cambrian Society, in 1829. His father, John Evans, was born in 1826. His mother's maiden name was Catherine Rowlands, daughter of William Rowlands, Agent of the Paris Mountain Copper Mine.

At the age of thirteen Fred entered upon a seafaring life. He was then a bright, active, muscular boy, quick to learn, and perfectly fearless of danger. He soon became thoroughly familiar with his duties. No old sea dog could " shin up " a rope quite as rapidly as Fred, and none was more ready to respond to every call of duty.

This period of his life, from the age of thirteen to twenty-one, was one of unusual hardship and danger. His first venture was upon the bark " Loraine," which was wrecked in the English Channel, and our sailor boy barely escaped with his life. His next venture was upon the steamship "Teutonia," which is unmarked by any important event. His second voyage, by the same steamer, was one of continued accident and danger. A fearful gale was encountered off the coast of Spain, the vessel lost her propeller, the sails were blown away, and for nine days the ship drifted at the mercy of the wind and waves. In endeavoring to land in small boats several of the crew lost their lives. A harbor was finally reached, repairs made, and the ship set sail for Havana. Before reaching its destination the propeller again dropped out, an accident which our young sailor foretold, and warned the Captain to prepare for, but his warning was unheeded.

But without attempting to follow him in all of his voyages, or note the many important incidents in his seafaring career, we will touch only upon the more important points.

In a voyage on the bark "Cynosure" from London to Australia, the cook, who had been acting strangely for several days, after preparing the evening meal ready for serving, jumped overboard and was lost. Lots were cast to supply his place and Fred was elected. On entering the galley to serve up the food, the dishes began to clatter and skip about in an unaccountable manner, and he fled in dismay to the deck; but he soon overcame his fears and returned to his task, when he found everything quiet.

It was during this voyage, in a fearful storm, that a wave broke over the ship, washing Fred overboard. A few moments afterwards, by the lurch of the vessel, or possibly by the aid of those powers which ever attend him, he found himself again on deck and uninjured. In fact, he seems, in his perils by sea, to have borne a charmed life, as we doubt not he did. The storm raged with great fury for many days. During its progress, when the crew were all on deck working for dear life to save the ship, he was sent into the forecastle on an errand. The place was quite dark, but light enough for him to see a strange man standing there, who showed him a knife wound in his breast, from which the blood was flowing. Fred noted his dress and appearance, but did not stop long to make his acquaintance! He told his shipmates what he had seen, and on the following day he was sent for by the Captain, and requested to recount his experience. He was informed that his description tallied exactly with that of a Spaniard who was stabbed and killed in a personal affray during a former voyage, and concerning which young Evans knew nothing.

This voyage lasted eighteen months, and was a series of accidents from first to last. He was warned by the invisibles not to ship in the vessel again, and although the Captain, who had treated him very kindly, urged him to do so, he refused. In her next voyage the ship was wrecked off Cape Horn, and all on board lost.

Our young sailor's next voyage was on the "Shatamuc" to New York. This vessel was water-logged, and for eleven days the crew were obliged to sleep in the rigging, where they subsisted on a cracker a day to each man, and a little water which they had been able to secure.

Evans is an expert swimmer, strong of limb, and perfectly cool in time of danger, qualities which have enabled him to rescue several persons from drowning. In March, 1881, a laborer fell from the dock in Bramley Moore, Liverpool, and would have drowned but for the timely assistance of Evans, who sprang into the ice-cold water and bore him to the shore. A few days later a man fell from the Husskisson dock, Liverpool, whom he also saved from drowning in like manner. But the most noteworthy incident of this kind occurred in April of the same year. Mr. Evans was a passenger on a steamer on an excursion trip on the River Mersey. There was a crowd of young people on board, who, on the return trip, and when nearing the wharf, became quite boisterous. One of the gangway fenders became displaced in their roystering, and a young lady was crowded overboard. Mr. Evans, who was standing in another part of the boat, on hearing the cry, " A man overboard!" was suddenly impelled by a mighty impulse to leap to her rescue. He did so, notwithstanding he was encumbered with heavy clothing. Seeing a white object floating near, he seized it. It was the form of the woman, who, fortunately for the brave swimmer, was insensible. It was ten o'clock in the evening, and the night was very dark. All was confusion on board, the boat was stopped and an effort made for their rescue. But they were lost in the darkness, and it was supposed that both were drowned. Evans bore up the fainting woman and manfully struck out for the shore, which he reached in safety. For this act the Liverpool Shipwreck and Humane Society voted him the thanks of the Society for his bravery, with a present of two pounds. The Society's certificate, which he has framed, is one of his most cherished treasures.

Mr. Evans' next venture was in an old bark in the cotton-carrying trade, which was wrecked in the mouth of the Mississippi River. Next, in the position of Quartermaster, on board the steamship "Arabic," he made a voyage from Liverpool, *via* the Suez Canal, to India, thence to China and Japan, and thence to San Francisco, where he was honorably discharged. He was afterwards engaged for two years as Quartermaster on various steamers in the coasting service, running to Victoria and other ports, and making two trips to Alaska. This ends his nautical career, which is quite enough for a young man then only twenty-two. He has some eight or ten honorable discharge papers, with several personal cards of merit, which he highly prizes.

In 1884 he commenced the investigation of Spiritualism, his first experience being at one of Mrs. Foye's public test seances given at Washington Hall, San Francisco. Venturing in there one evening, from curiosity, with a shipmate, his companion was dumfounded by hearing a name given known to no one present but himself, with a description of the manner of his demise, when, where, etc. Evans became much interested. He visited several psychics, all of whom assured him that he would be a powerful psychic himself if he would only sit for development. He finally concluded to do so, and after sitting every evening for about three months, and when about to abandon the effort in disgust, he received the gift of independent slate-writing, together with that of clairvoyance, clairaudience, and other phases.

The following account of Mr. Evans' psychical development is thus related by himself:

I first secured a pair of 5x7 school slates. I appointed my time of sitting from 10:30 to 11 every evening, for I was certain of being alone and undisturbed at that hour. The next plan was to make my room perfectly dark during my sittings. I might pause here and discuss the question as to why darkness was necessary, but I will not, further than to say that it seems a law of Nature that darkness is necessary in many of her most wonderful operations. The seeds of nearly all vegetable formations can only grow and mature in the midst of a profound darkness; and then, again, before they can germinate and grow, they must be covered with darkness and mother earth. The embryotic animal is unfolded and developed in the dark, and not until the form is fully perfected does Nature permit it to behold the light which thenceforward is its life sustainer. Why it is so none can answer. But that it is so all must admit, and so I found it in developing myself. I sat in my darkened room holding my slates for a half-hour each evening for two months, and never received a manifestation. I began to get discouraged, and determined that I should sit no longer for development, so I put my slates away and retired. I had been in bed about three minutes when I could see a bright luminous light at the foot of my bed. I thought it might be caused by the light creeping through the blinds and reflecting on the white door knob which was opposite the foot of my bed. Although I felt a little nervous I arose and hung my black coat on the door knob, so that it would not cause any delusion. I covered everything that was white with some black material. I next turned my attention to the only window in the room, and covered it so that not a ray of light could get in; the room was so dark that I could not see an inch before me. I groped my way back to bed, determined that if any light should appear it must surely be spirits. I had no sooner got into bed than several luminous lights were seen floating at the foot of my bed. Some would be about the size of a dollar and others would be about the size of a man's hand. I was determined to see in reality what they were, and was half out of bed with the intention of going to where the lights seemed to be located, when the lights suddenly came within an inch of my face. I jumped into bed and covered my head with the clothes to see whether I was being deluded in any way, when the clothes were suddenly pulled off the bed by invisible hands; forms floated about the room, and the whole room seemed to be filled with a white vapor. My bed began to shake, and loud raps sounded on the foot and head of my bed, then on the walls and doors. After standing this for about ten minutes I arose and made a light and smoked a cigar. After I had finished my cigar I felt more confident, and made up my mind that if I heard any more raps I would ask some questions. On retiring I again heard raps, and on questioning them learned that they wished me to continue my evening sittings, which I did, and from that date the rapid unfoldment of powers was marked. In holding the slates I felt as though I were holding on to a small battery. I then began to hear distinct raps on the slates, and a few nights later I realized that they were manipulating the crumbs of pencil I had placed between the slates, and after I had sat my usual time I found a number of small pencil marks on the slates. Each evening brought new developments, until one evening I found a letter "A" on the slates, and a few nights later I found the word "Patience" written on the slates; and so it went on every day improving, until in February, 1885, by the advice of my spirit friends, I gave up all other pursuits and devoted myself to the exercise of my mediumship as an independent slate-writer.

I found that each month improved my mediumship, and that one phase developed another, so that with my continued sittings I not only developed independent slate-writing but also automatic writing, rapping, clairaudience, clairvoyance, physical manifestations, and materialization, and have demonstrated all the above gifts to thousands in California. I gave my first public seance after sitting three months and a half for development. I found that darkness was only necessary during my sitting for development, and when I commenced to sit for the public, all my slate-writing manifestations were given in broad daylight, with the sun shining on the slates held in the investigator's own hands.

In February, 1885, Mr. Evans gave his first professional seance, since which time he has been constantly employed. At that time his means were exhausted, and it became necessary that he should receive pay for the exercise of his gifts.

On the twenty-first of June, 1886, Mr. Evans went before

the Society of Progressive Spiritualists, of San Francisco, at Washington Hall, where his guide, Spirit John Gray, produced over thirty messages, between a pair of sealed slates in the hands of a committee chosen by the audience. The slate is given herewith. (We may add that all slates appearing in this volume are reduced to almost three-fourths of their original size, excepting the one printed in colors.) The committee appointed to conduct this seance reported as follows:

> We, the undersigned committee, chosen by the audience at a public exhibition of independent slate-writing, given by Mr. Fred Evans at Washington Hall, on Sunday, June 21, 1885, testify that the slates used were washed and sealed in our presence and to our satisfaction, and during the time the slates were in use they were not removed from our sight. We distinctly heard the fragments of pencil between the slates writing, whilst holding them in our hands. When the writing was finished, which was denoted by three raps on the slates, Mr. R. B. Hall was selected by the audience to break the seals on the slates. When separated, one of them was completely covered with writing in patchwork form, embracing thirty communications, all in different handwriting. Each member of the Committee received messages signed by relatives or departed friends; the remainder of the messages was recognized by different persons in the audience.
>
> The exhibition was given in daylight before an audience of about 400 persons, and under conditions which excluded all chance of trickery or fraud.
>
> DR. THOS. C. KELLEY, 946 Mission St.
> MRS. F. C. LANE, 3010 Folsom St.
> WILLIAM KELLY, 202 Second St.

Again, at Scottish Hall, Mr. Evans did similar work worthy of note. At this latter seance a shrewd real estate operator, sitting in the back part of the audience, wagered twenty dollars with a companion that if he could be chosen as one of the committee to examine and hold the slates, no writing would appear upon the slates in his hands. Thereupon his name was called, and by vote of the audience he was elected as one of the committee. He examined his slates with especial care, saw hat they were thoroughly washed, dried and tied together, in a manner to make deception impossible. He did not suffer them

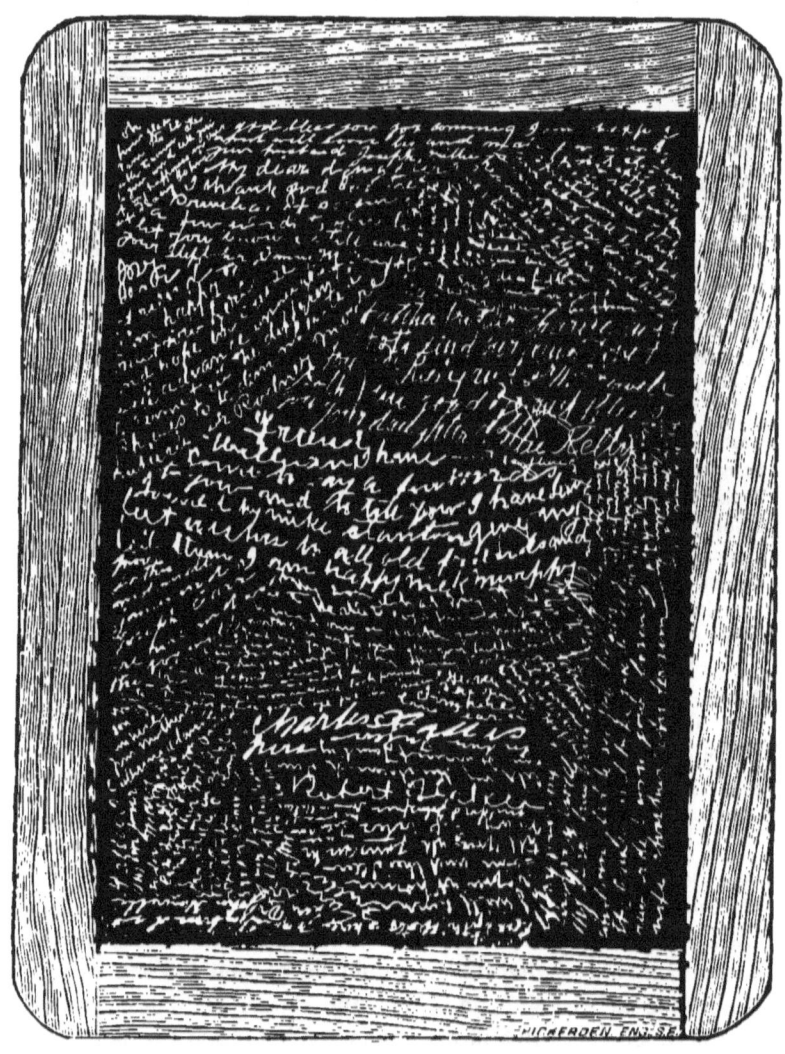

[Illustration given before a public exhibition through Fred Evans.]

to leave his hands for a moment, nor did Mr. Evans even touch them.

He declared that he heard the pencil scratching between the slates, and upon opening them one of the inner surfaces was covered with about thirty messages, written in the usual patchwork manner peculiar to this psychic. He gave it up, and was quite as earnest in extolling the fact as he was at first in declaring that it could not be done.

On the inner surface of one of the slates held by the other member of the committee, was also a large number of messages. It is needless to say that the friends of Mr. Evans were delighted, while the skeptics present were completely bothered.

FRED EVANS IN SAN JOSE.

IN the spring of 1887, the writer went with Mr. Evans before a large and intelligent audience in the City of San Jose, where, under crucial test conditions, he produced about eighty messages upon five slates—the slates being prepared and held by a skeptical committee. At a private seance, given for the benefit of the press, held on the preceding evening, there were present ten persons, all but one of whom had been or were then connected with the press. They examined and prepared the slates in their own way, held them in their own hands, and received some eight or ten messages written on four slates, most of which were of a private nature. One of the messages, written in red, white and blue, was from Spirit John Gray, and reads as follows:

> Good evening, gentlemen. I am glad to meet you here investigating this phenomenon. I hope you will speak of it as you find it, and not as you think, for you know that would not be treating the medium justly. Always be charitable, and your eyes will be opened to see truth and light, but bigotry will blind you. I will give each of you a manifestation soon that will add another item to the truth of spirit return. This from guide, JOHN GRAY.

Upon another slate "was found," as the *Times* report of the seance has it, "what purported to be a communication from the late Professor H. B. Norton, signed by him in a hand exactly resembling his signature." It reads as follows:

> I am pleased to give you these few lines as an evidence of spirit power. We do not wish to use too much of the medium's force to-day. But at an early date the medium will give you a better chance to hold communion with your spirit friends. I am pleased to have found that my old ideas of hell, etc., were unfounded, and that the realization of spirit return was true. Ah, well, I suppose in this city of churches, it will take a long time to make people understand this grand truth, but all will realize it some day.
> Yours in spirit, H. B. NORTON.

Upon another of the slates there were five messages, all of a private nature. The editor of one of the papers received a long message upon a slate held by himself, purporting to come from a friend in spirit life. Of this preliminary seance the *Times* says :

> We have complied with the request of the spirit boss to speak of it "as you find it and not as you think;" and our readers can do their own thinking on the subject to suit themselves. We have given the facts, and will only remark that anyone, having seen these phenomena, who should honestly attribute them to jugglery, ought to be placed in a "Home for the Feeble Minded," provided there were such an institution for adults.

The *Mercury* says of this seance that Mr. Evans "succeeded in mystifying all present," and adds: "There was no chance for sleight-of-hand, and nothing of the kind was attempted. The trick, if trick it was, could not be satisfactorily explained by the witnesses."

The public meeting, given at the Theatre on Sunday evening, drew forth the following cautious statement from the same paper:

> There was a large audience, and the introductory address was made by J. J. Owen, editor of the *Golden Gate*. A committee, consisting of S. A. Bishop, James T. Murphy, and Mr. Wolcott, was appointed, and several slates showed writing after being sealed up. A stranger from San Francisco brought his own slates, and he received communications upon them in writing.

To state the details of all that occurred at said meeting would occupy more space than we have to give to it. It may be sufficient to know that the committee prepared and sealed the slates in the most careful manner, never for a moment allowing them to leave their hands. A large number of messages was not only obtained between these slates, but one pair of large slates, securely fastened together and sealed, and brought to the meeting by a person in the audience, had both of their inner surfaces written full. One of the messages on these slates, from Spirit John Gray, was written in seven colors. Thus, six slates in all, containing about one hundred distinct messages, ranging from a few to as many as eighty words, were given, together with a fine likeness of Professor Hare, and all under conditions that would render deception impossible. Some of the messages contained several names, and nearly all of them were recognized by persons in the audience.

We give the following as a sample of the messages found within the sealed slates: (The first was written within the slate of a stranger present, who requested that writing be produced within his own slates.)

MY DEAR SON:—It is with feelings of the greatest happiness that I write these few lines to you. I know that it is hard for you to believe that spirits can come back and manifest for you in this manner. But you must admit of its truth when such evidence as this is given you. I know that you often will meet with opposition at your home when you accept Spiritualism as a truth. But you must know that its knowledge will make a happier and better man of you, for it will teach you to look forward to a brighter and better future. And the knowledge that those whom you love can see many of your acts will prompt you to do better things. I can see a bright future before you, Frank, my son, and will do all I can to prompt you in the right. This from your loving father in spirit, JOSEPH ZEPF.

This message was from the spirit father of the holder of the slate. Several of the following messages also appeared on this slate. Mr. Zepf had fastened the frames of his slates together at the corners with screws, countersunk the heads of the screws into the wood, and filled the places with sealing wax. Mr. Zepf declared to us that he had tried several times to obtain a sitting with Mr. Evans, but had always found him engaged. On learning that he was going to give a public seance in San Jose, he had prepared his own slates and followed him to that town, with the result as stated above.

I have come to assure my father and mother, whose names are W. C. and S. E. Wilson, that I have found a happier home in the spirit world.

JAMES WILSON.

To JUDGE BELDEN—*Dear Friend:*—I take this opportunity of thanking you for the kind and feeling remarks you offered in consolation to my family. This is true, Judge, although I know that you doubt it, but will find it out soon. *JUDGE McKEE.

* This prediction proved true, as in less than a year thereafter Judge Belden passed on to the other life.

Tell my mother and father, Mack and Mary Davis, that their son is happy.   ETHEL DAVIS.

I am overjoyed in being able to write a few words to you, just to acknowledge my presence. This from   ELIZABETH VINTER.

Tell my papa and mamma, and brother Alden, that their little son, Josie Anderson, is here.

The spirit of Mary E. Chase sends love to her husband.
J. W. CHASE.

To MY MOTHER, OLIVIA, AND MY FATHER, S. H. AMBLER—*Dear Parents:*—I am so happy to find that I can write and assure you of this grand truth of spirit return. This from your son,   FRANK A. AMBLER.

The spirits of Mary Ellen and E. L. Bradley wish to be remembered to their loved ones left behind.   E. L. BRADLEY.

To MY SON, A. J. CORY:—My son, I am joined with your mother, Eliza Ann, and sister, Adalina, and Susan Williamson, in sending love to you and your brother, Ben. Your son, Bertie, is also here and sends love to yourself and to your dear wife.   Your father,   J. M. CORY.

The names and relationships of these spirits were recognized as correct.

Charles, my boy, I am pleased to write a few lines to you. I hope you will not be afraid to acknowledge this truth, for all will realize it sooner or later.   JAMES AND MARY SHORTRIDGE.

To E. S. HARRISON:—I have been waiting anxiously for the time when I could manifest through you alone, for I know by that means I could convince many of a future life, and of the power of spirits to return. I must tell you that you will soon hear of news that will benefit you, both financially and socially. This from the spirits of   ELIZA AND E. HARRISON.

The spirits of Mary and James Shively send best wishes to R. O. Shively, with assurance of their happiness in the spirit world.

It gives me great pleasure to come back and prove to you that I am not parted from you forever; but that we will meet again to part no more.
ARTHUR DELACY AND MARY DELACY.

DEAR DAVID:—I and our children, Nellie and Lutie, send love to you. This from your loving wife in spirit,   NELLIE WILLIAMS.

Tell my husband, Rev. Amos Jones, that Spiritualism is true. His wife,
HELEN JONES.

Please tell Mr. E. O. Smith that Elizabeth and James Smith are with him in spirit.

Father dear, I am with you in spirit, though I am absent in body.

EMMA GORDON.

Give my love to my father, Ira Moore. From his daughter in spirit,

CAROLINE MOORE.

MY DEAR MAMMA:—Your daughter, Cecil, is here, and happy in her spirit home. I am joined with Grandpapa Cornelius Huyck in sending love to you. This from your loving daughter, CECIL BAIRD.

The spirit of Davis Divine wishes to be kindly remembered to the dear ones he has left behind.

We give but a few of the scores of messages upon these slates, some of them written so fine that they can scarcely be deciphered. They consist mainly of loving greetings, with names of those who have passed on to the other life. It is the fact and manner of the writing, rather than the character of the message, in which the public will naturally find the greatest interest. That there was any chance for deception, or that there was the slightest suspicious circumstance attending this remarkable exhibition, no fair-minded person present will aver. The committee chosen by the audience to prepare and seal the slates were most thorough in their work. They are honest, just men, who would stand no trifling or nonsense in a matter of this kind.

The San Jose *News*, of March 14th, and the *Times*, of the 15th, give long and very fair reports of this meeting, the latter journal copying many of the messages received, and describing the careful manner in which the slates were prepared by the committee, and all confirming the essential facts herein set forth. It is not so much the communications themselves as it is the manner in which they are produced, that concerns the public.

We will add, for the information of those present who discovered some errors in names, and also a similarity in the chirography of the messages, that it is not claimed that the writing was done in each or any instance by the spirit from whom the message purports to come. Until the spirits learn to control the conditions themselves, they must necessarily write through an amanuensis. We have found that with practice they soon learn to write for themselves, and then the messages come in their own handwriting. (Spirit " John Gray " explains this matter in an able article written by himself further on.) The spirit father of the writer, also a wife and brother in spirit life, from each of whom we have had many communications through various psychics, have mastered the conditions and invariably write in their old, familiar hands.

Of the exhibition as a whole, we venture to say that it is unparalleled in the history of modern phenomena for its conclusive demonstration of spirit power.

[Obtained through the mediumship of Fred Evans at a public séance given in San Jose, Cal., April 2, 1887.]

PSYCHOMO LODGE.

FRED EVANS is one of the few psychics of our acquaintance who, in addition to his peculiar gifts, possesses fine business qualities. By careful ventures and investments, coupled with his psychical work, he has secured for himself a fine home in San Francisco, valued at some $20,000; also a beautiful resort in the Santa Cruz Mountains, with a neat little cottage and six acres of choice fruit land planted to trees. Thither he goes with his family for rest and recreation, when his nerve forces need the baptism of rest and the re-invigorating touch of nature.

The following article, by the writer, in the *Golden Gate*, written on the occasion of a visit to, and the dedication of, Psychomo Lodge, may not be out of place here. It is entitled, "The Beautiful Hills:"

"The Coast Range of hills south of San Francisco affords an unending variety of charming locations for rural homes. The soil is the best in the world for general fruit culture, and the climate unsurpassed for healthfulness and equable temperature, and there are cosy little nooks, here and there, with patches of landscape—glimpses of mountain, lake, valley and sky—that no art can imitate, no pen describe.

"Just such a gem of a place is this hitherto unnamed brochure of the Santa Cruz hills (this day, Sunday, June 15, 1890, christened 'Psychomo Lodge'), the property of our psychographic friend, Mr. Fred Evans, where the writer and wife, with their genial hosts, are spanning, with a rainbow arch of glory, a couple of restful days.

"I wish I could describe the scene that spreads out before me from the open doorway where I pen these lines. First let me say that, about three years ago, Mr. Evans purchased six acres of wild hill land, located on the westerly margin of one of the

San Jose Water Company's mountain reservoirs, about two miles from the Alma Station, on the South Pacific Coast railroad. About four acres of this land were at once cleared of the brush, brought under cultivation, and planted to choice fruit trees. A neat cottage was erected on a charming little plateau overlooking the lake, a place that nature seems to have designed especially for that purpose, and thither the owner comes, at times, for that rest and recuperation he needs to supply the exhaustive waste of vitality, caused by the practice of his mediumship.

" Psychomo Lodge is distant only a three hours' run from San Francisco, and the trip may easily be made after business hours, with an hour to spare for black bass fishing in the clear deep waters of the lake. (And here I will say, parenthetically, and as a sort of background for the sketch I hope soon to attempt, that this reservoir forms a lake about thirty acres in extent. The water is deep, pure and sparkling, and is one of the sources of water supply for the City of San Jose. Of course, it is private property, with all the rights and hereditaments thereunto belonging, of which the right to fish therein is one, but which right may be temporarily waived, in favor of any good citizen, for a small fee, to him in hand paid, the faithful watch and warden of the place, Mr. Wm. Chilcote. This fee includes the use of boats, fishing tackle, etc. Were it not thus, the lake would soon be despoiled of its finny tenants by the kingfishers of the cities, and the limpid waters thereof be desecrated by the unwashed elements of society.)

" Overlooking this beautiful body of water, at an altitude of about one hundred feet, sits Psychomo Lodge. Beyond the lake, and to the right and left, are rolling hills, hooded with green vineyards and orchards, and dotted with the cheerful and pretty homes of the inhabitants. Beyond, and about two miles distant, a remarkable depression in the inner rim of hills skirting the far-famed Santa Clara Valley, opens the eager and penetrant gaze to that Elysian vale of beauty and industry, where sit enthroned, with clasped hands, the royal Saints Jose and Clara. On and on, across this exquisite plane of twenty miles of farms and orchards, rises the other rim to the valley—a cloud bank of hills in the shadowy haze of distance, gray and mellow, as the mountains that uplift themselves in the soft twilight of our dreams. Highest and most conspicuous among these gray billows of land, Mt. Hamilton raises its proud head, garlanded with stars, and the white dome of the great Observatory flashes back to me an echo of the persistent query of my longing soul, What? Whence? Wherefore?

"This view, one of the grandest that ever ravished the eye of sense, and which nowhere else in all this range of mountains can be equaled, lies before me, on this bright June day, a panorama of marvelous beauty. Surely, some good angel must have guided our Fred's footsteps to this delectable retreat.

"Perhaps it was the magnetism of such grand natural scenery as this that inspired the brain of the gifted young daughter of Mrs. Belle Baker, a near neighbor of Psychomo Lodge, to catch the golden threads of the sunsets, weave them into shapes of beauty with the gray, purple and green of these Beautiful Hills, and impinge the creations of her fancy upon canvas. Miss Ada is a close and careful student of the art she loves so well. She has done some excellent work, and will yet do greater things in the coming years.

"Last evening, as the sun sank behind the western hills, and the twilight shadows began to temper the summer's fervid glow upon the waters of the lake, our party, intent upon a fish banquet, glided out in a small boat to try their luck. A dozen fine bass rewarded our efforts, most of which were caught by—one of us! Later on, a friendly piscatorial odor stole upon and permeated the evening air from the kitchen, and still later several discarded spinal remembrances of the feast, with their accompanying side bones, were pitched into the waste, and we arose with a blessing upon the Infinite Energy that invented black bass! Really, the fish are fine and fat, a fact which is apt to weaken the tenure of their existence.

"Would that we could take these outings oftener—once a week would not come too often. Every brain worker needs them to get the best out of himself; for there is no strain upon the energies like that of hard thinking. It uses up the oil of life as in a furnace, and the brain and spirit need reoxidizing and revivifying with the fresh breath of the forests and hills, and a new impulse from the magnetic batteries of our good mother, Nature."

EXTRAORDINARY PHENOMENA.

DR. JOHN ALLYN, an old and honored physician of St. Helena, California, wrote the following article for the *Golden Gate:*

EDITOR OF *Golden Gate:*—I deem an account of the following extraordinary phenomena worthy of record in your paper, not to advertise the medium, though he is certainly worthy of his fee, but to encourage truth-seekers and skeptics to investigate for themselves.

On the third of May, I purchased a pair of new slates and took them to the rooms of Mr. Evans. It was mid-day when we took seats opposite each other by table. I had previously cut one of the initials of my name on the frame of each slate. Unwrapping the slates and looking again to see that they were clean, I handed them to Mr. Evans, who took them and tied them together with wrapping twine, then sealed them with sealing-wax in the four places where the twine crossed the frames and also where the twine was tied; a bit of pencil was placed between, previously. I then, after writing three names on a ballot, which was folded up and placed on the slates, took them in my two hands. Mr. Evans took another slate and washed it clean, threw it upon the carpet about four feet from us, with a bit of pencil beneath. Soon the table seemed to be charged with some invisible force, as there was a fusillade of small raps. Soon I heard the writing between the sealed slates, which continued for about fifteen minutes, when three raps from the inside of the slates indicated that the writing was finished. Mr. Evans asked how many messages were written on these slates, and there were four raps. I then raised the slates from the carpet and found the under side written full and signed "Matthew Allyn." Without opening the slates I put them in my valise and brought them home. I called in a few friends, among them two editors of weekly papers. I explained how the writing was done; stated that I was certain there was no writing when the slates were sealed, and that I was confident there were four messages signed by different parties, two of whom I knew, and two I did not know. I said one would be signed by my mother, and one by Swedenborg, as I had placed these names written on a ballot and folded closed upon the slates. I then cut the twine, opened them, and found the surfaces covered with four messages, one signed by Swedenborg, one by Clara Allyn, one by J. Allyn, and one by E. Allyn, his wife; the two latter passed away forty years ago.

In the writing there are evidences of the identity of the writers, but to point them out would make this article too long. JOHN ALLYN.

ST. HELENA, CAL., May, 1886.

CHALLENGE.

ST. HELENA, Cal., May 18, 1886.

For the purpose of stimulating investigation into the significance of certain slate-writings had by the undersigned on the third of May, 1886, with Fred Evans, I make the following offer: To any sleight-of-hand performer who will show that said writings were done by trickery or fraud, or will do the same on equally test conditions and explain the same, $1000. To any scientist who will do the same by any forces known to science or any law unknown to science hitherto, and prove the same, $1000. In all of these cases the fact and hypothesis of Spiritualism must be excluded.

JOHN ALLYN.

The challenge has never been accepted, and is not at all likely to be.

A SLATE OF MANY LANGUAGES.

FRED EVANS is a great home body. Although his name and fame are world-wide as a slate-writing psychic, he rarely leaves San Francisco, notwithstanding the great demand for him from all parts of the world. We accompanied him once on a professional tour to the southern portion of California, his wife going with us; and once, with his wife, he visited Australia, remaining for more than a year, whereof we shall speak hereafter. It is more difficult now than ever for him to leave home, as he is the proud father of two beautiful baby girls, to whom, with their mother, he is deeply devoted.

Most of our experiments in psychography with Mr. Evans were procured at his own home. Such was the case with the remarkable slate, a *fac simile* of which we present in this connection.

This slate, which has been copied in nearly all of the spiritual papers of the world, as well as by many secular papers, which we regard as the finest instance of psychography yet given to the world, was obtained in the presence of the author and his wife.

Mr. Evans is a young man with only a moderate English education. No one who knows him believes him capable of writing such a slate as this; and to suppose that the various writings and languages could have been placed thereon by persons competent to do the same, would be to suppose that such educated persons would become parties to a stupendous deception, involving the crime of forgery. The history of this slate is as follows:

In September, 1886, the author having in contemplation the publication of a holiday number of the *Golden Gate*, called

[Slate of twelve languages, produced under absolutely test conditions through the psychic power of Fred Evans.]

upon Mr. Evans, accompanied by his wife, for the purpose of consulting with him, or rather with his psychographic guide, Spirit John Gray, concerning the preparation of a slate, that we could have engraved, which should bear upon its face some intellectual evidence of genuineness; as any slate, written in English, no matter how crucial the conditions under which it was prepared, would be positive evidence only to those *knowing* to the facts.

Our first interview was on Sunday, September 11, 1886, at ten o'clock A. M. Besides the invisibles, only the three persons above mentioned were present. Sitting at a table, in the full light of day, Mr. Gray instantly signaled his presence by raps upon the table, when we explained to him our object, inquiring if it was possible for him to bring together a number of spirits of different earthly nationalities, who could furnish us short messages in their native languages. He replied that he thought he could do so, answering our questions either by writing independently, by telegraphic rapping (which Mr. Evans has learned to read), or by writing automatically through his instrument's hand. He at once entered heartily into our plans.

It was found, as has usually been our experience when sitting with psychics for this phase, that our presence afforded a strong assisting battery, and that the writing came with great readiness, three and four slates being written upon simultaneously, and all without the slightest attempt at concealment.

The controlling influence requested that we meet Mr. Evans at the same hour for a few Sundays, and hold the same slate, when he could more fully determine his ability in the matter. We placed a private mark upon the slate, which we had then held for a few minutes, and it was laid aside until the following Sunday.*

---

* In captiously questioning the genuineness of this slate, a son of the eminent psychic, D. D. Home, says we did not state that our private mark was still upon the slate after the mes-

On the second Sunday writing came freely upon other slates lying upon the table, and upon some placed on the floor near where we were sitting, but none upon the slate under our hands. Mr. Gray assured us that he was getting along finely—that he was sure he would be able to procure writing in several languages. He recognized the excellent conditions we furnished him, and expressed himself as greatly pleased with the experiment.

On the third Sunday, September 25th, we were promptly on hand, as before. The slate containing our private mark was taken by Mr. Evans and first thoroughly rubbed on both sides with a cloth slightly dampened with his saliva—(not a very neat way of cleansing a slate, but Mr. Evans says the writing comes much more readily when the slates are thus prepared). He then handed the slate to us, and we (Mrs. Owen and the writer) were both fully satisfied that there was no writing upon the slate. From that moment the slate never left our hands, nor was it for an instant out of our sight. A small bit of slate pencil was placed upon the table, and we placed the slate over it, with our four hands resting thereon. Mr. Evans, sitting upon the opposite side of the table, touched the outer edge of the slate frame for a few moments, and then removed his hands entirely. In about five minutes loud raps signalled that the writing was finished. We raised the slate and found the under side covered as seen in the engraving.

Two other slates, which had been prepared in like manner and placed upon the floor, with a bit of pencil between, were found at the close of the seance written full. As the message purports to come from the controlling spirit, and relates to the main work in hand, we give it:

---
sages were written, an omission which we will here correct. The mark was and is still there. Another criticism, by Wm. Emmette Coleman, was that the Greek was not the kind of Greek written in the days of Socrates. Spirit John Gray explains that the Greek of the Ancient Grecians is necessarily passed down through the brains of modern spirits of that nationality, until it is finally impressed upon the brain of the psychic's guide, who gives it to the best of his ability. So it is with all languages with which he is not familiar.

My Dear Friends, Mr. and Mrs. Owen:—I see your object is to create an interest among skeptics of spiritual phenomena and cause them to investigate. I entered in with your feelings, and have succeeded in inducing twelve spirits of different nationality to write a few words in the language they used when on earth. You will, no doubt, find many defects, but we have done the best we can, and you must accept it with the knowledge that these spirits never wrote through the medium before; therefore, they are at a disadvantage; and there is also a difficulty in bringing them here to write, for, as you will understand, there is no attraction for them. But I have the medium, yourself and wife, for an attraction. You will see that the languages written embrace Chinese, Japanese, Egyptian, Old Asiatic, Hebrew, German, Italian, French, Spanish, Greek, Norwegian and English. Wishing your dear wife, yourself and the *Golden Gate* every prosperity, I am your friend and well wisher in spirit, John Gray.

Of the messages given there are some defects, as Mr. Gray says may be expected; but on the whole we regard the writing as most remarkable, the Asiatic languages especially, of which but very few of our own race have ever acquired anything more than an imperfect speaking knowledge. A learned professor, who assisted in the translations, thinks there is not a scholar in San Francisco who can write all the languages given upon this slate. Following are the translations of the writings:

German—I have found an easy way for making known to science the proof of the return of the dead to this earth, and I shall soon give it to the world. Professor Zöllner.

Italian—I am glad to be able to write you a few lines to aid in proving the truth of a future life. Count Rozzia.

French—*Monsieur Gray:*—I have acquitted myself of your commission. M. Fremont.

Greek—I come to say this—seek for better things—think well of all. Socrates.

Spanish—*My Dear Friend, Sr. Don Owen:*—Rich or wise as a man may be, don't let him be proud. It is from a King, Agesilaus, we have that grand maxim, "that one is not great only as far as he is just." Don Juan Alviso.

Norwegian—I am here.—Herr Holle.

Chinese—I write a few words for you.—Lu Yeun.

JAPANESE—How do you do?—OYAMA GENTURA.

HEBREW—[This is a name of a book, describing the killing of animals according to the Jewish rites.]

The writing in the upper left hand corner is claimed to be Egyptian, which we were unable to translate. We submitted the matter to John Gray, when he wrote the following: "I give it to you as received by me. The Egyptian reads : 'Yea, the spirit of man shall live forever.—NEFO;' who was an old Egyptian seer."

The cuniform characters just below the Egyptian comprise the letters of the words "Tom Paine." *

MY DEAR FRIEND MR. OWEN:—I have succeeded in bringing the above spirit friends together and inducing them to write a few words in their earthly language, as a test of spirit return. This is the best we can do. Good-bye.

JOHN GRAY.

To set at rest any idea that may be entertained that this writing was a transference from our own minds, we will say that with the exception of some little knowledge of French and less of Spanish, the English language is the only language with

---

* The key to these cabalistic characters is given thus:

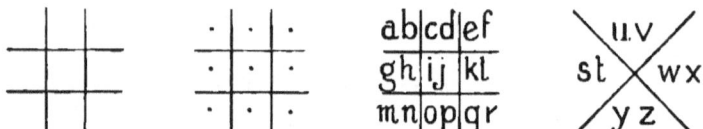

The first letter of the English alphabet is made thus: ⌐, a; the addition of a dot constitutes the second letter, ⌐, b, and so on to the end of the alphabet. With this key the writing is easily read. For illustration, "Tom Paine" is written thus:

T O M P A I N E

These cuniform characters are demonstrated by a learned writer in the *Medium and Daybreak* to be of great antiquity. Their adaptation to the English language is, of course, a modern affair.

which we are familiar. We positively *know* that the writing was not done by any mortal hand. As we have in our possession the slate upon which it was written, any one interested can satisfy himself that the writing is by no chemical preparation, as the fine particles of slate caused by the attrition of the pencil over the surface of the slate can readily be seen.

We have given, in the above statement, the simple facts; the skeptical reader may explain them as best he may.

We desire to call attention to some evidence of genuineness of this slate other than that of those who witnessed it and *know* that the writing was done by no mortal hand.

Of course, we do not claim that the messages were written in each instance by the spirits of the persons from whom they purport to come; in fact, we are inclined to think that most of them may have been written by the psychographic guide of Mr. Evans while under the psychological control of said spirits —just as a German spirit, for instance, might influence a sensitive who had no knowledge of German, to speak or write that language. It would naturally be more or less imperfect. It is the *fact*, and not the *nature* of the writing, in the manner claimed for it, that we desire to establish.*

Now, the skeptic will naturally insist that we were deceived—that the slate we held in our hands, and upon which we know there was no writing, was not the slate that we found in our hands at the conclusion of the seance, and upon which the writing appeared—that in some mysterious way the slate was changed in our hands.

Let us, for the sake of argument, assume that this was the case. Then, the writing must have been placed thereon by

---

* It is the imperfection of many of these messages that has led various critics, ignorant of the law governing the transference of thought on the spirit side of life, to question their genuineness. The late Colonel Bundy, editor of the *Religio-Philosophical Journal*, fell into this mistake, as did also the son of D. D. Home, and others. The intellectual quality of a message from the spirit side of life must necessarily take more or less coloring from the brain through which it is conveyed—just as a ray from the sun is colored, and often deflected, by the glass through which it shines.

Mr. Evans, or by persons familiar with the languages written. As for its being the work of Mr. Evans, no one who knows him believes him capable of doing anything of the kind. He was a young man of twenty-four when those messages were written, evidently unschooled in any language but the English, and only indifferently well in that. He had certainly, while residing in San Francisco, never been heard to utter a word in any language except his own.

This writing implies a classical education, which Mr. Evans surely has not. In fact, it is doubtful if there is a single individual in America who can write in the twelve languages named. There are probably many who can write in more languages, but not in those twelve. Hence we are obliged to dismiss the supposition that the writing was done by Mr. Evans.

Then, if not written as claimed, who could have done it but various persons in the community qualified to write said languages? And just here we encounter a difficulty which all must readily appreciate. Would an intelligent German, Spaniard, Italian, Frenchman, Norwegian, etc., be apt to lend himself to such a fraud and commit actual forgery by signing another's name to a written message? Don Juan Alviso, for instance, a former well-known resident of California, addresses a personal note to the author, with whom he was acquainted. Would any sensible and intelligent Spaniard, as the writer of that message evidently is, be apt to sign Alviso's name to a message of that kind?

If these messages were written by any persons in mortal life, they must certainly know it; and they must now know that we have published to the world the claim that the writing was produced by some occult power. We now invite, yea, challenge them, in the interest of truth, to come forward and disprove the claim.

As confirmatory of the genuineness of the writing upon this slate, we might refer to a slate, given in this connection, and which contains fifteen messages. This slate was written at a seance given to the writer and a number of personal friends, nearly all of whom were strangers to Mr. Evans. The slates were prepared and sealed by a committee from the audience. They were wound with cord and suspended to the gas jet in the centre of the room, Mr. Evans never touching the slates from the moment they were placed in the hands of the committee, and yet all but two persons present received messages thereon.

There were present at this seance fourteen persons in all, besides Mr. Evans and his wife. Six of those present were entire strangers to the psychic, who also had no previous knowledge as to the proposed attendance of any members of the circle, with the exception of the writer and two others. There were no ballots written, and care was taken that the names of the strangers present should not be made known to Mr. Evans. Therefore no introductions were had; nevertheless, all present, except two, received messages upon the slate, some receiving two and three. The names given of the spirit friends of the persons unknown to Mr. Evans are a most convincing test of spirit power.

The manner of the writing was as follows: A committee of two was appointed to see that the slates were properly cleaned and sealed. This was done first by thoroughly rubbing the slates with a damp cloth, and then, after placing a few minute bits of pencil between them, they were sealed together with sealing-wax at the edges. The committee then tied a cord around the slates and hung them to the gas jet in the centre of the room. In a few moments the rapid moving of the pencil tips was distinctly heard, and in about four minutes light rapping announced that the writing was completed. The committee then removed the cord and seals, when the inner surface of one of the slates was found written over, as seen in the engraving.

Some of the messages show carelessness of construction; but no more so, perhaps, than they would if written by a like number of mortals of average intelligence. The messages show

[Given through the mediumship of Fred Evans, at a select seance of personal friends of the author.]

distinct styles of chirography. And what may be regarded as a significant fact is that, as far as known, the writing is the same in appearance as that given by the same spirits through other slate-writing mediums.

Take, for instance, the message in the left upper corner, signed "Josephine." (The word closely resembling "Mother," in the address, was "Mattie," in the original, the name of the wife of the author—evidently a mistake of the engraver.) Mrs. Owen has received messages from her sister Josephine through three psychographists—one in New Orleans—and the writing was alike in all instances. Such, also, is the case with the message in the right hand upper corner, purporting to come from the spirit father of the author.

The profile sketch in the lower corner to the right, is not a bad representation of a life-size bust of the writer's spirit father, by Anderson, in possession of the author.

That the writing in the above instance was produced in the precise manner we have stated, fairly and without collusion of any kind, all present at the seance will affirm to be true. One evidence of its genuineness is conclusive in this, that Mr. Evans could not have known who were to be present, for that was a secret with the writer; hence, there could have been no previous preparation of the slates. Another is in the fact that he never touched the slates after they had been prepared by the committee.

Mr. Evans' powers have been tested by thousands of persons, and often under the most crucial test conditions—sometimes producing the writing within riveted slates, and frequently without the contact of hands.

A few months prior to producing this last slate Mr. Evans was happily married to Miss Agnes Hance, a sensible, intelligent and handsome young lady, who now devotes her attention mainly to the cares and duties of motherhood, while her husband exercises his wonderful gifts.

SPIRIT ART.

THE sketch from which the likeness of the late D. D. Home was engraved (as it appears herewith) was procured in the following manner:

We asked Spirit John Gray—the psychographic control of Mr. Fred Evans—if he could not induce some spirit artist to furnish us with portraits and sketches from the spirit side of life for publication in the *Golden Gate*. With the same alacrity as that with which he undertook to procure messages for us in various languages for our holiday number, he entered into our plan.

Owing to the illness of Mrs. Evans the date of our first seance had to be postponed. We called upon Mr. Evans, in company with Mr. John Waterhouse, lately of Minneapolis. Mr. Gray had advised us not to sit with others during the process of these experiments, hence he was a little dubious at first as to the result, but was soon pleased to proceed with his work, as our friend was found to be a help rather than a hindrance.

A single slate, that we saw thoroughly cleaned upon both sides and wiped dry, and which we were permitted to handle, and knew for a certainty contained no writing or mark of any kind, was placed over a small bit of slate pencil on top of a table. We held our hands upon this slate for a few minutes, when the control asked for a bit of lead pencil, which was passed under the slate, and we continued to sit as before. In about ten minutes raps upon the table signified that the work was done. Upon turning over the slate we found that its under surface had first been evenly whitened by the attrition of the slate pencil, and upon this whitened surface appeared the likeness in crayon, together with the names at the bottom, that of D. D. Home being a perfect *fac simile* of the hand-writing of that eminent medium.

Mr. Gray informed us that the sketch was made by a spirit artist, but that the writing was done by Mr. Home himself.

SPIRIT D. D. HOME.
[Obtained through the psychic power of Fred Evans.]

SEANCE WITH PROF. A. R. WALLACE.

THE most remarkable seance in many respects for independent writing with Mr. Evans, was one given in presence of that eminent scientist, Professor Alfred Russell Wallace, F. G. S., of England, his brother, Mr. John Wallace, of Stockton, California, Dr. David Wooster, one of San Francisco's leading physicians and a member of the Academy of Sciences, and the writer—four persons in all besides the psychic, Mr. Evans.

We arranged for this seance with Professor Wallace, to come off at nine o'clock in the morning of the day mentioned, at the residence of Mr. Evans. It was fully half past nine when we reached his residence, where we were pleasantly received by Mr. Evans, and conducted to the seance-room, which was a small front room directly over the hallway. The morning sunlight was streaming in at the window, and the room was as light as noonday.

Mr. Evans took a seat at a table with his back to the window. Professor Wallace and his brother sat at the opposite side of the table, Dr. Wooster sat behind the Professor, and the writer, behind and a little to the right of Mr. John Wallace, the object being to give the brothers the fullest possible benefit of the seance.

A pair of medium size folding school slates, brought by John Wallace, who had never witnessed any experiments in psychography before, was placed upon the table, together with two pairs of other slates, and, a few minutes later, a single slate, with cross lines thereon to indicate that the colored writing usually produced in this experiment is written over the cross, was placed upon the table. The slates were all thoroughly cleaned and examined by the brothers, and were, from first to last, directly under their hands and sight.

Without giving the experiments in the order in which they were produced, or even reproducing the numerous messages written (as they were mostly of a private or unimportant character), we will speak more especially of the *manner* of their production.

As we have frequently described in this volume, the messages through this psychic are always given under what may be regarded as absolute test conditions. All being done in the light and above board, with the slates in the hands of the investigator, there is not the slightest suggestion or possibility of deception. And such was the case in this instance.

The influences worked readily, and in a few minutes several messages were written in the ordinary way, to the delight of Professor Wallace, who expressed his admiration of the prompt and perfectly fair manner in which they were produced.

The Professor then inquired of Mr. Evans if writing could be produced upon paper placed between the slates, when he was requested by the spirit control to tear off six sheets from a common writing pad of white paper at hand and place them between a pair of slates, which he did. In a few minutes we were assured by the psychic that the forces were at work upon the paper, and soon it was found that upon each of five of the slips of paper was a finely executed crayon sketch of a prominent Spiritualist passed to spirit life, representing them as they appeared in earth-life, viz., D. D. Home, Dr. Benjamin Rush, Dr. Robert Hare, Jonathan Pierpont, Mrs. S. F. Breed, and upon one slip an unknown spirit picture not as well done as the others.

It is a significant fact that these five sketches named were improved copies of pictures taken upon the slates upon former occasions by the spirit artist, Stanley St. Clair, through Mr. Evans' powers, and who also drew upon a slate, at this seance, the picture of Father Pierpont, which we reproduce in this connection. (The artist produced this picture at our reporters' seance in Los Angeles, and it was retained by one of the reporters present.) And yet it was seen that the crayon sketch of the latter was not an exact copy of the slate picture produced at this seance. If it is of the former picture we have no means of knowing. They were all, with the exception of the spirit picture referred to above, pronounced by Professor Wallace to be artistic and meritorious sketches.

Perhaps the most remarkable test given at this seance was the writing in five colors, by Mr. Evans' control, produced on the under side of the slate with the cross, the writing appearing *over* the white lines. The colors used by the spirit in this experiment are remarkably brilliant. In fact it is the best sample of colored writing we have yet seen through this psychic. The message reads as follows:

DEAR FRIENDS:—I am pleased to meet you all here, and to you, Professor Wallace, I must express my deep admiration for the noble stand you have taken in bravely advocating that which you believe to be true, namely, the truth of spirit return. Alas! too many are bound down to accept that which they do not believe in, merely because it is not fashionable to doubt it. I mean orthodoxy. But the time is fast approaching when all will only be too glad to embrace a belief in Spiritualism. I must leave you now with the glad thought that I will one day welcome you all to the spirit side of life.

Spirit guide, JOHN GRAY.

Another most remarkable experiment was given as follows: Mr. Evans placed a sheet of white paper over a slate lying upon the table, upon which slate it was seen there was no writing. He raised the slate level, touching his forehead with the edge, when in less than half a minute there was found upon the upper surface a finely written and beautiful message of one hundred and forty-seven words, signed "Elizabeth Wallace," the name of a sister of Professor Wallace. This message must have been almost instantaneously stamped upon the slate, and yet the writing is, to all appearances, the result of the attrition of a slate pencil over the surface of the slate.

The last, and, to the scientist, perhaps the most satisfactory experiment of the seance, was the production of writing on the two inner surfaces of the folding slates brought by Mr. John Wallace. Upon one surface was a message by Spirit John Gray, and upon the other a message signed "T. V. Wallace," the name of the father of Professor Wallace. This writing was absolutely conclusive of the existence of an independent occult intelligent power capable of performing such wonders.

We will add, in conclusion, that a slate placed upon the floor contained four short messages to the author—one from John Gray, the others from three spirit friends, and in a *fac simile* of their familiar chirography. The number of slates written over, including the one with the picture, was eight, containing in all thirteen written messages, which, with the slate picture and six crayon sketches, we consider the most remarkable result ever obtained at a single seance with any slate-writing psychic. The duration of the seance was less than one hour.

The above appears to me to be a correct account of one of the most remarkable and convincing seances I have ever attended. I have never, on any occasion, witnessed phenomena of so wonderful a character appear with such rapidity and in a manner so entirely free from suspicion.

ALFRED R. WALLACE.

I agree with the above remarks of my brother.

JOHN WALLACE.

I entirely agree with Professor Wallace in his estimate of the phenomena and the perfect freedom from any suspicion of fraud in their production.

D. WOOSTER.

We will add to this chapter some very interesting experiments of our own with Mr. Evans. We may say that such perfect harmony of conditions has been established between us that the intelligences manifest themselves with a readiness and power that is ever a source of surprise, even to us who have witnessed so many exhibitions of spirit power.

On one evening with Mr. Evans, the writer and his wife

[Taken independently, between closed slates, through the mediumship of Fred. Evans, at a private séance. Note to Professor Alfred R. Wallace, May 27, 1887.]

each took a couple of slates which we knew were perfectly clean. We tied them together in pairs, writing our names on the outside of each slate.

We then left the light and entered the dark cabinet with Mr. Evans, taking the slates with us and never for a moment allowing them to leave our hands. In the cabinet Mr. Evans sat in front of us, with his right hand resting upon the left hand of one of us, and his left upon the right hand of the other.

The light was extinguished, when immediately loud raps upon the floor, the chairs and the slates, announced the presence of the invisibles. Soon a small, luminous cloud formed near the side of the psychic, which took the shape of a beautiful human hand, which floated down, first over one of the pair of slates, and then over the other, and seemed to be writing upon the upper surface of the slates. Detaching one hand from the slates we were holding, we were permitted to take this luminous hand in our own. We found it cold and firm—very like the hand of a living person just out of the cold.

Another interesting phase of this seance was the materialization and illumination of a slate which was held before us with the name of the guide, John Gray, written thereon in large, luminous letters. A small piece of pencil was also illuminated and caused to write rapidly over the surface of a slate. The scratching of the pencil was loud and distinct, and its rapid movement over the slate was witnessed by all with deep interest.

It should be remembered that throughout these experiments, the slates prepared by us were held in our own hands, and that the psychic's hands never left ours except to enable us for a moment to take the spirit hand before him. He was not entranced, and enjoyed the seance quite as much as did we.

Upon entering the light we found no writing upon the outer surfaces of the slates, except that of the names we had placed there; but on the inner surface of one of the slates was a message from John Gray, in common slate pencil writing, and on one of the inner surfaces of the other pair of slates were thirty-three shades of colors, put on as with a fine brush, in lines three-fourths of an inch in length; and then, stretching lengthwise across the slate, was a belt an inch and a half in width made by an interblending of all these shades. Some of these shades are exquisitely delicate and beautiful, and the coloring matter lies in small ridges upon the slate. Below the colors was written in pencil: " Mr. Owen—Dear Friend—We have given you this to show you how easily we can produce all colors when necessary.—JOHN GRAY."

THROUGH SOUTHERN CALIFORNIA.

IN the spring of 1887, Fred Evans made a professional tour to the principal towns of Southern California. He was accompanied by his wife and the author—the latter acting as a sort of business manager, or major-domo. The trip throughout was one grand in its consequences as an educator of the people in the mysteries of psychic science. Of the trip down we wrote as follows to the *Golden Gate:*

" It is indeed grand to live in such an age as this—an age of wonderful things—of the triumphs of steam, of electricity, of spiritual and intellectual unfoldment. How unlike the dreamy past in everything save in the operation and workings of Nature's unchanging laws. Had some fairy said to us in the long ago, when early manhood, with its rose-tinted hopes and eager ambitions, first dawned upon our life, and our dreams of the future were bright and golden with the glory of being, ' My son, the evening of thy days and of a busy life will be spent in a land by a far-away sea, devoted to the spread of a religious philosophy that shall have for its basis the positive proof of the existence of the spirit of man as a conscious entity beyond the gateway of death,'—had some fairy or prophet said this to us, it would have seemed a monumental fiction. So, too, it would have seemed to the bright young sailor boy of a half dozen years ago, had some priestess of the future predicted that erelong there would come to him a gift, upon the marvelous demonstrations of which the world would look and wonder. How truly we can say—

'God moves in a mysterious way
His wonders to perform.'

"A trip by sea from San Francisco to San Diego has been

too often told, and is really of too humdrum a character to be interesting. It is, perhaps, enough to say that the steamers are the best of their kind, with all the modern conveniences; the officers are polite and efficient; the tables are excellent, and, to the lasting credit of the managers, be it said, there is no bar on board—that abominable nursing school of drunkenness and vice! Not that wines and liquors may not be had upon application to the steward, but they are not set constantly before one as a temptation to the young and idle. We have noticed that it is usually the old toper, or the moderate drinker on the down grade, that ever orders his poison by the bottle.

"Drifting out upon the ocean, though but for a brief journey—away from the tear-dimmed eyes of those one loves—away from familiar faces and scenes—out upon the rolling waste of waters—a plaything of the waves—it is so unlike a journey one takes by land that there is always a touch of sadness in it for me. It is so typical of the journey we must all take, sooner or later, over the dark waters whose billows break forever on the silent shores of Death. And yet I enjoy a voyage by sea as I never do a journey by land. I love to be rocked to sleep upon its mighty bosom. One can get nearer to the Infinite Heart upon the ocean than upon the land, for it is there one must necessarily feel more dependent upon the sustaining arm of the Infinite One.

"We left San Francisco at two P. M., Sunday, April 3d (Mr. and Mrs. Fred Evans and the writer), stopping a brief while the following morning at Port Harford, and by two P. M. of the same day we were at beautiful Santa Barbara, where we tarried for six hours. Here we were met by a committee of the saints, and a carriage placed at our disposal for a ride about the city. Mrs. Evans was presented with a basket of elegant flowers, and our stay in the city was made most delightful. To those stanch and true standard-bearers of the gospel of Spiritualism, Brothers Maxwell, Barber, and Morris, and also to Mrs. Morris, we owe our heartfelt gratitude for a brief season of delight. We drove out to the old Mission Church, and out and in among the pretty villas of the town. The boom of improvement was here, as everywhere else along the Southern Pacific Coast, and the sound of the hammer and the saw makes rich melody in the ears of the festive land-owner who has lots to sell.

"Another long stop at San Pedro, and a few hours later we are at San Diego, where lots are selling for $40,000, more or less, with the climate and bay thrown in! Five years have elapsed since my last visit to this city, and behold the change! The city has more than doubled in population during that period, and is at present extending in all directions. Magnificent business blocks and elegant private residences are springing up on every side, and that good time coming, of which the ancient San Diegan so fondly dreamed, seems at last to be here. Well, we rejoice in her prosperity. After all, what can there be attractive about a home or a country where life is made a constant agony between summer's heat and winter's cold, or where the gaunt specters of Fever and Pestilence brood over the land?

"In the face of the ignorance, prejudice, and defiant skepticism prevailing everywhere concerning our facts, it is no light undertaking to go before the public and attempt to *prove* the truths of Spiritualism. We know of no psychic in the world to-day who can face this skepticism so grandly as can Mr. Fred Evans, and demonstrate the slate-writing phase of the spiritual phenomena.

"Upon the evening following our arrival here, twelve representatives of the press met at our rooms and were given a private test seance by Mr. Evans. Eleven of the number present received messages from their spirit friends within slates prepared, sealed, and held in their own hands. While seated around the table Mr. Evans placed a cross upon the surface of a slate that all saw had first been thoroughly cleaned, and then, under their own eyes and hands, a message was written thereon in four colors, the writing showing plainly where it crossed the white lines that it was written *over* the cross. Other equally astonishing evidences of spirit power were given, and all declared, through their respective daily journals—the *Union, Sun, San Diegan*, and *Bee*—that they could detect no deception.

"Our first public meeting was given at Leach's Opera House, and notwithstanding a heavy rain-storm prevailed there was a goodly attendance. Three slates full of messages were obtained, and one slate with a fine likeness of Dr. Rush. Upon the latter slate also appeared eight messages to members of the audience. There were fifty-four messages in all, from a single name up to a message of fifty and sixty words.

"One of the gentlemen upon the committee chosen by the audience—a Mr. Welden—stated that he had been before the public as a performer of legerdemain, and that if it was a trick he had witnessed it was the finest 'upon the boards' to-day. He showed to the audience how he and others of his profession produced what they called spirit writing, and declared that Mr. Evans' writing was done in no such way, and he was unable to tell how it was done!

" The pair of slates first sealed and held longest by the committee contained no writing, a circumstance which another member of the committee could not understand. Neither do we, although we might present a theory therefor which all enlightened Spiritualists would understand. Time was required to harmonize the conditions and prepare the way for the writing. The positive conditions surrounding the first slate made it easier for the spirits to write upon the slates that were prepared and sealed a few minutes later, perhaps.

" It is not a question of the ability of the spirits to overcome all hostile elements or magnetism; but rather, can they produce writing under any conditions ? If committees will be reasonably passive and receptive to the truth, Mr. Evans' psychographic control, John Gray, will give them all the evidence they need.

"At the second meeting Mr. Welden, the gentleman mentioned herein (who is a fair and honest skeptic, by the way), brought with him his own slates, declaring that if he could get the writing thereon, he would publish it in all the daily papers of San Diego. Mr. Evans invited him to call at his rooms at ten A. M. on the following day and bring his slates, and he would see what his guides could do for him. He came at the appointed time, and received a message within his slates from a loved sister, written in her own hand. At the meeting of the First Spiritualists' Society, of San Diego, on Sunday morning following, Mr. Welden was present, and made a public statement of the fact. He also caused the same to appear in the daily papers. Mr. Welden is a prominent contractor and builder there; he is a gentleman of culture, and well known as a thoroughly honest and upright man.

"In our work in San Diego we obtained some rich experiences which will prove valuable to us hereafter. We found there, as we do everywhere else, that the claim of a spiritual source for the intelligible messages received upon the slates, arouses the bitter hostility of all those who would have it otherwise. The arrogant, opinionated skeptic, who cannot by any means discover the *trick* (as he considers it), finds his sagacity overmatched. He is humiliated in his conceit and pride of superior knowledge, and it makes him angry. The ignorant and thoughtless readily fall in with their intellectual (not moral or spiritual) betters, and are ready to create disturbance when admitted to our seances.

"At our second meeting there was quite an attendance of the rougher elements, who evidently came for a disturbance. It was half an hour before order could be restored. An excellent committee, consisting of Dr. Goss, Mr. Gilman, and Mrs. Bellamy, was finally secured, and, notwithstanding the nervous condition of the psychic, consequent upon the inharmony aroused at the outset, the influences worked readily and almost immediately. Six slates were obtained, containing some fifty messages, including a fine picture by Spirit St. Clair, and interesting experiments by the psychic's guide, Spirit John Gray, and also by the spirit of Professor Norton, who is deeply interested in our work. The latter comes to us frequently, his messages being invariably a *fac simile* of his well-known chirography. As when on earth his messages are models of English composition. He produced the writing, in the above instance, upon a wet slate just taken from a bucket of water, and which had to be dried before the message could be read. Upon a close examination the writing was found to be produced by the attrition of a slate pencil upon the surface of the slate. John Gray produced writing in colors *over* a white pencil cross upon a slate prepared, sealed, and held by the committee. Indeed, the manifestations were most astonishing, far exceeding those obtained at our first public meeting in San Jose.

"As we were advertised for only two public meetings here, under the instruction of the guide, the remainder of our stay was devoted to private seances. And at these seances some of the medium's best work has been done. The sitters, in nearly all cases, brought their own slates with them, and never failed to find them written full. In several instances the bottom and two inner surfaces of the slates would be found written over, and all without the contact of mortal hands. It should be remembered that Mr. Evans never removes the slates for a moment from the sight of the sitter. When not under the sitter's hands, or lying upon the table, they will be placed upon the floor or mantel, but always in plain sight. The writing comes with wonderful power and directness."

Speaking of the seance given to the San Diego reporters, the *Union* of that city said:

Whatever may be believed of the cause of these manifestations of power of some kind, they were certainly wonderful. The utmost alertness was unavailing to detect any trickery. Mr. Evans even made crosses on the

SPIRIT PICTURE.
[Taken through the mediumship of Fred Evans, before a public audience in San Diego, and under the supervision of a committee chosen by the audience.]

slates, and these were found to be written over instead of under, as would have been the case had there been chemicals or invisible writing upon the slates. An unusually sharp lot of eyes watched proceedings, and found no cause of complaint. It is certainly worth seeing, to say the least.

The San Diego *Daily Bee* also had the following:

At a seance given by Mr. Fred Evans last evening for members of the press of San Diego, the following message, written in four colors—red, blue, yellow and white—was received by C. Y. Benjamin, business manager of *The Bee*, and one of its two proprietors:

I give you these few lines as a test of spirit power, and I wish to assure you that your present undertaking will prove a success, for it will lead you to better things. Wishing to add another item to this truth of spirit return, I remain yours in spirit, J. BENJAMIN.

The slate upon which this message appeared was thoroughly cleansed with a dampened sponge and then rubbed dry with a cloth. The medium then took a pencil and made two large and distinct marks on each side of the slate in the form of a cross, and stated that the message, if one appeared, would be written in four different colors and *over* the marks in white made by the slate pencil. Placing a small bit of pencil upon the table, the slate was laid over it. A moment afterwards the slate was picked up by Mr. Evans and the above communication disclosed.

Messages were also produced upon the inner surfaces of two sealed slates, laid upon the table, under the watchful eyes of all present, no hands touching them except those of the five gentlemen of the press, selected to see that no juggling or sleight-of-hand tricks were indulged in. *The Bee* representative had a back seat, and so cannot be accused of putting up a job on his less fortunate brethren of the quill. Upon another slate, cast upon the floor some distance from the medium, ten messages were quickly produced by some mysterious agency, and when read to the assembled gatherers of news, each one was found to have received a brief communication. Another slate was filled with a communication, signed by H. B. Norton, late principal of the State Normal School, at San Jose. Another slate, placed upon the mantel and out of the reach of Mr. Evans, was also filled with writing.

The San Diego *Sun*, of April 7, 1887, published the following:

REMARKABLE PERFORMANCE AT A TEST SEANCE LAST EVENING.

A private test seance was given last evening by Fred Evans, the slate-writing medium, at which representatives of the press were present by special invitation. Many mysteries mankind may never solve, or at least be able to satisfactorily explain, and the performance of Mr. Evans last evening may fairly be classed among them. The slates used were thoroughly wiped dry, and placed in various parts of the room. Four slates were sealed together in pairs and placed upon a table in the centre of the room, and given in charge of five newspaper men. The following messages were written upon the slates. * * * * * *

Those present at the seance were Messrs. Rogers and Hildreth, of the *Union;* Messrs. Bacon and Julian, of the *San Diegan;* Colonel N. L. Vestal and E. N. Sullivan, of the *Sun;* Harr Wagner and wife, of the *Golden Era;* J. J. Owen, Mrs. Clara S. Foltz, Mr. Clinkscales and C. Y. Benjamin. Whatever trickery there may have been it was not evident—no one present could detect it. Mr. Evans will give a public seance at Leach's Opera House this evening, when his psychographic control (spirit of John Gray) will undertake to produce messages from the spirits of departed friends, between sealed slates prepared by a committee chosen from the audience.

FRED EVANS AT LOS ANGELES.

WE reached the City of the Angels in the midst of a drenching rain. Not only the windows, but the doors and skylights of heaven seemed open, so great was the downpour. But we could rejoice with all Southern California in the aqueous blessing, for it meant a bountiful harvest in the coming days.

Los Angeles, we doubt not, was at that time the liveliest city of its size on the continent. From a population of 10,000 a decade before, it then numbered 50,000, and was increasing at a rapid rate. Eastern capital was flowing in there a steady stream. Fine business blocks and beautiful homes were springing up in all directions, as by the touch of the magician's wand. And what mightier magician is there, in the temporal affairs of life, than money? It can move mountains into the sea, and make an earthly paradise of a desert waste. But this Los Angeles country was never such a waste. Here and round about is some of the finest land in the world—a soil as rich as that of the Valley of the Nile, and a climate as soft and genial as that of the Grecian Isles. This is, indeed, a land of sunshine and flowers—a land where the olive and the vine, the orange and the fig, flourish in perfection, and where human life can find more natural enjoyments than in any other spot of earth under the twinkling stars. This stupendous fact the Eastern world is beginning to appreciate.

Spiritualism, in Los Angeles, was just then at a low ebb. There was no organized society of Spiritualists there, and no regular meetings were held. An occasional speaker entered the field as a sort of free lance, but unless of commanding ability there was apt to be a "beggarly array of empty seats." This was from no lack of spiritual elements, for the believers in our philosophy there were numerous. It is the old story of inharmony, caused mainly by disagreements in matters of phenomena. There is enough upon which Spiritualists can agree, it would seem, to enable them to maintain an effective organization, in any community with one-fourth the population of Los Angeles.

The Unitarian minister there, Dr. Fay, was such an able expounder of spiritualistic teachings, in all except the evidence of a future life, and was such a grand soul withal, that many Spiritualists were pleased to attend upon his ministrations. And we cannot blame them, for he preached the true gospel of humanity and brotherly love. While listening to him on Sunday morning (he speaks at the Grand Opera House to immense audiences), we could not help thinking that if the good brother could only give his hearers something more tangible than a barren *hope* of a future life—if he could assure them of a verity that death is but the gateway to another and better world—to a life of unending progression upon another stage of existence—if he could bear to them the gospel of this glorious truth, how the hungry hearts of many of his hearers would rejoice.

Man wants the positive proof of another life. The Christian world believes in it through faith, but faith will not answer satisfactorily the question, "Whither, oh, whither has my beloved gone?" The grief-stricken mother, who lays the form of the darling babe, that death has plucked from her bosom, away in the cold grave, is not content with the blind and undemonstrated assurance that it will be tenderly cared for in some far off heaven. She must *know* that it has found a shelter in the loving heart and home of some ministering angel—some mother spirit in the Summer Land.

But then there is so much aversion in many minds to everything savoring of Spiritualism—they are so afraid of the name—that we are inclined to think that Brother Fay was doing more good than he could do as an avowed Spiritualist. He was certainly reaching a class that he could not reach as a minister of the gospel of Spiritualism; and his followers were being led into the spiritual fold without knowing it.

Our first seance there, given to the reporters of the daily press, was, as usual, a grand success. The leading dailies were all represented, and the reporters expressed themselves as thoroughly mystified. Unlike our first reporters' seance, held in San Jose, the writing commenced almost immediately after the slates were cleaned and sealed, and the manifestations were of a most satisfactory character. The crucial test of writing in colors *over* the lines, an oblique cross drawn upon a slate with a slate pencil, was given by Spirit John Gray; and Spirit Stanley St. Clair produced a fine crayon likeness of Father Pierpont; all of which was done upon slates in the hands and under the sharp eyes of the reporters.

Concerning this seance we copy the following, entitled "Odic Forces," from the Los Angeles *Herald*, whose reporter was present:

Representatives of the press were last night invited to attend a seance, or display of odic forces, by Mr. Fred Evans, a most remarkable medium, about twenty-four years of age. Mr. Evans is of Welsh descent, and for a few years was a sailor before the mast, from which position he rose to that of quartermaster. A little over two years ago he made the acquaintance of Mr. J. J. Owen, formerly the iconoclastic editor of the San Jose *Mercury*, in Santa Clara County, who became deeply interested in the remarkable medium, and accompanies him in his travels and exhibitions.

By request of Mr. Owen, Mr. Kemp, of the *Evening Express*, Mr. Madrill, of the *Daily Tribune*, and a representative of the *Daily Herald* attended the seance last night at the rooms of Mr. Fred Evans, on the corner of South Main and Fourth Streets. Mr. Evans is a very pleasant gentleman of graceful manners, slight physique, and a powerful medium of the unseen forces that act with terrible energy on the human mind. The representatives of the press saw all the movements of a mechanical nature, but not the movement of the hand that wrote the communications and made the artistic representations.

A slate, clean and free from all marks except an X that extended across it, made with a common slate pencil, was laid on the table and sealed to another clean slate, with a small piece of white pencil laid between them. The three representatives of the press laid their hands upon them for a few minutes, when, upon opening them, by breaking the seal, the following sentiments were written, in ten different colors, over the cross lines, each line containing only one color:

To the Gentlemen of the Los Angeles Press—*Dear Friends:*—I am pleased to meet all here this evening to witness this phenomenon. I know that many of you would like to bear witness to the truth of spirit return; but, also, too many are afraid that their belief would be ridiculed and scoffed at by their many friends. All that I ask is a fair report of their test of spirit power, for by so doing it will encourage us to give you more proofs in the near future of your spirit friends. This from the medium's guide. Good-night. John Gray.

The spirit of Stanley St. Clair was asked to make a picture, and produced a good likeness of John Pierpont, the poet, while the slate was firmly held by the three representatives.

About the portrait of John Pierpont was written the following:

Dear Friends of Los Angeles:—You who have it in your power to spread this knowledge of spiritual nature, I have drawn this spirit picture of John Pierpont for your benefit, and on representation of the press, and if you will speak of it as you see it you will amply repay yours in spirit, artist, Stanley St. Clair.

The spirits also sent, through the medium, the following communications of a personal nature:

Tell Joe that Dan Lynch is here in spirit and will write him more soon.

My Dear James:—I am glad to see you here investigating the grand truth. Tell all the dear ones that I am happy. Mary Ayers.

To James J. Ayers:—God bless you. It is with feelings of happiness and joy that I come back to write these few lines to you. I know you often doubt the possibility of spirit return, but I will soon prove it to you beyond a doubt. You know there is much in this belief to make your stay on earth happy, for it will cause you to look forward to a brighter future and to a happy reunion with friends gone before. I am joined with James, Joseph and William in sending love to you from the spirit of Elizabeth Ayers.

Please tell Jay that the spirit of Elizabeth Hanchett is here. Jay can tell his wife that Bud and Max are here. H. Hanchett.

The spirit of Henry Osborne, also his mother, too, is present.

I have come to tell you all that there is a life after death, and that it is not as bad as your preachers paint it. Wm. McFarland.

Tell John that I have come to assure him of my happiness in spirit life.
W. J. Davies.

The spirit of G. Otis is present.

I have come to make my presence known. A. Eastman.

Please tell Willie Spalding that I am with him in spirit, though absent in body, and that I hope soon to demonstrate my presence to him at his own home. May Spalding.

Jane Cleveland wishes E. R. to know of her happiness in the spirit world.

On Sunday night we appeared before a large audience at the Grand Opera House. After a brief address by the writer, an able but skeptical committee, of which ex-Mayor Spence was a member, was chosen. They proceeded with the utmost caution to clean and seal the slates, never allowing them to leave their hands for a moment. A few minutes only elapsed when the committee was requested to break the seals. Some twenty-four written messages to persons in the audience were found within the slates. Each member of the committee stated the above facts, and declared that he did not know how the writing came there. Other slates were written, and a fine likeness of Mrs. Breed was given by the spirit artist, St. Clair. Other slates would doubtless have been written over but for the inharmony caused by some unreasoning skeptics present, who were unwilling to trust the investigation to their own committee.

We are pleased to note that Mr. Evans' psychic powers are increasing. The writing, before a public audience, comes much more readily than at first. Through his wonderful gifts the world will be convinced of spirit power as never before; for through him the truth can be presented in a manner to sweep away all doubts. At his private seances, in nearly all instances, investigators bring their own slates (single and double and of all sizes), and they invariably get them written full.

After our public seance in Los Angeles, a juggler named Ausbach published a card in one of the local papers, in which he claimed to expose Mr. Evans by insisting that he used false bottoms to his slates. We replied to this through the same journal as follows:

MR. AUSBACH'S "EXPOSÉ."

COLONEL OWEN'S DEFENSE OF THE SLATE-WRITING MEDIUM.

EDITOR *Express:*—Will you kindly permit me a few words in reply to Sala Ausbach's explanation (?) of Mr. Evans' method of independent slate-writing, as published in your issue of Tuesday evening?

SPIRIT PICTURE OF MRS. BREED.

[Taken through the mediumship of Fred Evans, at Child's Opera House, Los Angeles, the slate being held upon the head of Mr. Bliss, a member of the committee selected by the audience to prepare and hold the slates.]

We are surprised that so "well-known and expert a juggler" as Mr. Ausbach claims to be, should attempt to impose upon an intelligent public that ancient "fake" of a false bottom to the slates, as an explanation of the writing witnessed by your reporter at our rooms on Saturday evening last, and also by the Los Angeles public at the Opera House on the evening following. Does he not know that the very first thing any intelligent committee would look for would be said alleged "false bottoms?" It is certainly not very complimentary to the discernment of the competent committee chosen by the audience, nor to the sharp-eyed reporters of the Los Angeles press, who had every opportunity to demonstrate the fallacy of the "false bottom" theory, to assume that they could be so easily duped.

At the reporter's seance, one of the very best tests given was upon a single slate in the hands of the gentlemen present—the writing appearing in colors *over* the lines of an oblique cross placed upon the slate. Would they not have been apt to detect the cheap trick, and have branded Mr. Evans as he deserved to be, had he resorted to any such silly deceptions?

We can give the names of twenty respectable and intelligent citizens of Los Angeles, who have come to Mr. Evans' rooms during the present week, bringing their own slates (double and single and of all sizes), all of whom have obtained the writing thereon under their own hands. In no instance has there been less than two, and in one instance as many as eight slates, written full.

In the light of this fact, what becomes of Mr. Ausbach's "false bottom" theory? It looks very much as though the aforesaid "expert juggler" was endeavoring to obtain a little free advertising at the expense of Mr. Evans' reputation.   Very respectfully,   J. J. OWEN.

Los ANGELES, April 21, 1887.

CHALLENGE ACCEPTED.

The following also appeared in the *Tribune* of that city:

EDITOR *Tribune:*—In your issue of this morning, Mr. George L. Wilson, assuming that the writing produced under the hands of the committee at the Opera House on Sunday evening last was a "chemically-prepared slate trick," says, over his own signature:

I will buy two slates and put them in the hands of the same committee, and if Evans & Co. can write one word on either of such slates I will pay them $1000. I will put the money in the hands of the committee.

While Mr. Evans cannot, of his own skill or volition, produce one word between closed slates, he is willing to try the experiment proposed. As we must leave for Santa Barbara on Saturday morning, the experiment must take

place as soon as possible; but no extended time is needed for preliminaries. Mr. Wilson will please deposit his $1000 with the committee (of which Mr. Spence, of the National Bank, is a member) at once, and arrangements will be immediately made for the seance. Should the experiment prove a success, we will leave $100 of the sum in the hands of the committee, to be distributed among the poor of Los Angeles at their discretion. J. J. OWEN,
Los ANGELES, April 21, 1887.   Manager for Fred Evans.

It is needless to say that "Mr. Wilson" was never more heard from.

Concerning Fred Evans and his work, the Los Angeles *Express* contained the following, entitled

THE SPIRIT WORLD.

A Clever Exhibition of Ghostly Skill—Colonel Owen's Protege—A Young Sailor Who Became a Medium—How He Did It—Seance with Skeptical Reporters—They Go Home Mystified—Entertainment at the Grand Opera House.

Colonel J. J. Owen, erstwhile editor of the Santa Clara portion of the northern citrus belt, the San Jose *Mercury*, arrived in this city on Thursday, and on Friday afternoon visited this office and informed the editor that, if convenient, he would like a reporter to be detailed to visit his rooms at the Montrose, Saturday night, at eight o'clock, and there witness an exposition of what is known in spiritualistic circles as "independent slate-writing," the placing of two slates together, with a bit of pencil between them, by a medium, the laying on of hands by the spectators, and the visitation of an alleged spirit who inscribes messages upon them.

The medium who claimed to be possessed of this wonderful power, Colonel Owen said, was a young man named Fred Evans. Accordingly, Saturday evening, an *Express* reporter knocked upon the door of room eighteen, at the Montrose. A voice answered, "Come in," and the scribe, entering, found himself in a very cozy apartment, and standing in the presence of an extremely youthful looking and handsome man, attired in a neat suit of black, of well-cut features, and possessed of a dashing pair of clear, large black eyes.

"A reporter, aren't you?" he asked, and being answered in the affirmative, he said: "I thought so. You see, I told Colonel Owen to invite the members of the press, that I might show them what I could do, before my formal appearance at the Opera House to-morrow night."

Then Mr. Evans (for it was the medium himself) showed the reporter a chair, and the two, sitting opposite each other at a pine board table, were soon conversing. The conversation naturally turned to the medium himself, and in response to queries of the *Express* man, Mr. Evans, in a very agreeable way, related the following of himself and his career.

[Here follows an account of Mr. Evans' early life and development as a medium, which has already appeared in this work, and which we omit here.—THE AUTHOR.]

Evans told this story without any of that display characteristic of so many so-called mediums, and in a manner that would generally carry to an auditor the conviction that he was speaking the truth. At nine o'clock Mr. Berry, a *Herald* representative, and Mr. J. W. Maddrill, of the *Tribune*, entered. Evans announced that he would proceed with the seance, and then directed the " pencil pushers " to arrange themselves around the table, and they did so. Colonel Owen, himself, took a seat next to the *Express* representative, Mr. Maddrill sat to his left, and Mr. Berry next. Evans' seat was directly opposite his audience, across the table; then, at the medium's request, a most minute examination was made of four common school slates, about 4x6 inches in size, framed with pine wood usually used in slate manufacture. After the slates had been inspected, Evans took from the box a slate pencil and scratched the surfaces over with it. He then spat on them, cleaned them off, and then handed them again to the newspaper men. They were as of yore. Taking two of them and placing them together, Evans dropped a bit of pencil between them, and then sealed them together with common red sealing wax. The same performance was gone through with the other two slates, and, laying one pair above the other on the table, the medium directed all four persons to place their fingers upon them and "arrange a battery;" then the little party sat in silence, and awaited coming events. Evans assumed an easy position in his chair, and very shortly signs of his laboring under a severe mental struggle were made apparent. He writhed and twitched his fingers, and finally grasped a pencil and commenced writing upside down, with lightning-like rapidity.

"He has heard them," whispered Colonel Owen as Evans finished.

Turning the paper about one could readily decipher the writing. It was in words as follows:

Yes, I will write on the slates to the press. JOHN GRAY.

"Who's John Gray?" was the simultaneous inquiry of the newspaper men.

"He is Mr. Evans' 'psychographic' control; more properly speaking, the medium's guide in the spirit world," was the whispered response of Colonel Owen.

At this moment the grating of the bit of pencil between the two uppermost slates could be distinctly heard, and in a moment Mr. Evans had ordered hands removed. He picked up the slates and handed them to Mr. Maddrill, at the same time requesting him to force the slates apart. Maddrill did so, and on the top slate of the two were written, in excellent chirography, the following messages:

[We omit the messages, as of no particular interest in this connection.—THE AUTHOR.]

One of the slates was then thoroughly washed in water, all present at first tasting, and, found pure, was placed on the table, and between it and the table board was placed a bit of pencil that had been used on the slate just examined. On this single slate the party placed their fingers, the same mental struggle in Evans was apparent in a moment, and he quickly inquired, in hollow tones, " Is that you, Johnny ? " With one accord the trio of reporters glanced at Colonel Owen. " He is asking for his spirit control," was his response. " Is that you ? " continued Evans. " Well, will you show the reporters that what we believe is truth, by writing on this single slate, after I mark it with a cross, by writing across and over the cross I place on it— will you ? "

Then Evans grasped a pencil, and in the same way he did before wrote a few words. Inverted, they read, " Yes, I will." Evans then quickly picked up the little slate, and with a bit of pencil drew two lines on it crossing each other obliquely over the surface. It was then replaced, and the scribes' fingers, with those of Colonel Owen, were soon upon it. In a remarkably short space of time the grating noise was heard. Evans, when it ceased, ordered the slate lifted, and, to the intense wonder of his audience, there upon its surface was a message, its letters written in colors of purple, red, green, blue, and white, over the cross Evans had placed upon it. So much were they amazed that nothing but " Ohs! " and " Ohs! " were uttered for several moments.

"That I consider my best demonstration of the proof that spiritual power exists," said Mr. Evans, as well he might, triumphantly. The message, in its parti-colored writing, read as follows:

To THE GENTLEMEN OF THE LOS ANGELES PRESS—*Dear Friends:*—I am pleased to meet you all here this evening to witness this phenomenon. I know that many of you would like to bear witness of the truth of spirit return; but, alas, too many are afraid that their belief would be ridiculed and scoffed at by their friends. All that I ask is a fair report of this test of spirit power, for by so doing it will encourage us to give you more proofs, in the near future, of your spirit friends. This from your medium's guide.   Good-night.
JOHN GRAY.

After a most minute examination of the table, the furniture in the room, its walls, ceilings and windows, the party gave up the solution of what they thought a problem, when Mr. Evans said he would, if possible, endeavor to communicate with the artist spirit, Stanley St. Clair.

At once the party returned to their seats. The *Express* reporter cleared off a slate, and it was placed as had been the one on which was the cross. Hands were then laid upon it, and in less than three minutes Mr. Evans had a communication with St. Clair, his artistic spirit. He wrote upon a paper what St. Clair had to say. The unseen delineator said he would, for the press, draw a picture on the slate, and in a few minutes Evans lifted the slate from the table. Engraved upon it in slate pencil was a likeness of John Pierpont, the poet—an artistic bit of work. About the portrait, in legible hand, was written the following:

DEAR FRIENDS OF LOS ANGELES:—You who have it in your power to spread this knowledge of spiritual nature, I have drawn this spirit picture of John Pierpont for your benefit and at the request of the press, and if you will speak of it as you see it, you will amply repay

Yours in spirit,
ARTIST STANLEY ST. CLAIR.

Evans' auditors were thoroughly mystified. It was inexplicable, unfathomable. Mr. Evans, as the party retired, smilingly bade them good-night, and asked specially that they attend his performance at the Opera House.

AT THE OPERA HOUSE.

Four hundred people gathered in the Opera House to witness Evans go through his slate-writing manifestations. Ex-Mayor Spence, Mr. Jesse Yarnell, and O. H. Bliss were chosen a committee to scrutinize his work. The manner of preparation was exactly the same as used at the reporters' seance, detailed above, and of course the committee left the stage more mystified and as ignorant of Evans' *modus operandi* as they were when they went upon it. Considerable excitement was created, and when Colonel Owen and his protege, Mr. Evans, retired, the audience became a noisy one. The entertainment was a successful and mystical one, and Evans was dubbed an "artist."

The Los Angeles *Times*, who, by the way, was accidentally omitted in the press invitation seance, and consequently felt a little sore, has the following to say:

About 400 people gathered at the Opera House last night to attend the seance of Fred Evans, assisted by J. J. Owen, late editor of the San Jose *Mercury*. Evans is a young man, and was met by Owen some months since, who thought he had discovered a most wonderful being. In consideration of the row that was kicked up last night, and quelled by Owen, it might not be out of place to give a brief history of that gentleman. For twenty years Owen was a prominent citizen of San Jose, and was sent to the Legislature from Santa Clara County some years ago. Mr. Owen entered the newspaper business soon after he took up his residence in the Garden City, and during the twenty years of his residence there, he was an able advocate of the principles of the Republican party. He built up the San Jose *Mercury*, and when he disposed of that paper, about two years ago, it was the best-paying newspaper property in the State outside of San Francisco. Mr. Owen's friends, and, in fact, the whole Republican party of Santa Clara County, objected most strongly to his disposition of the old party paper, and a number of the local leaders of the county met the gentleman, and almost begged him not to leave them at that particular time. It was just before the last Presidential campaign, and Mr. Owen finally consented to remain until after the election, but he could not consent to remain any longer than that, for a new life, or a new set of ideas, had taken possession of the venerable editor, who had made a State reputation, and he could not give up the army of cranks who had thrown their nets around him. His friends had noticed for several years that he was becoming a strong believer in Spiritualism, and they feared that he was throwing up his useful calling to add his influence to the shadowy ranks. Their conjectures proved correct, for, after taking a trip to Honolulu, Mr. Owen started a Spiritualist paper in San Francisco, called the *Golden Gate*, and since then he has been a strong supporter of the mysteries of the "spirit land."

Mr. Evans is a very young man, who does not look as though he is yet out of his teens. His every action shows that he has been a hard worker in the peculiar profession he has adopted.

Soon after the audience became seated at the Opera House last evening, Owen appeared on the stage, and announced that the circle was completed, and the seance would begin. He made a neat little speech, and was frequently applauded by the believers present.

The slates at this seance were all carried away by the excited audience, but the success was similar to that witnessed at other places.

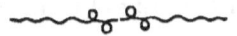

OUR PSYCHIC IN SANTA BARBARA.

AS compared with the mad rush and whirl of business life of Los Angeles and San Diego, Santa Barbara presented a picture of quiet repose. Here were to be seen many of the sleepy old relics of Mexican architecture—the one-storied, tile-roofed, ungainly *adobe* structures of a past age; but they are rapidly melting away before the advancing tide of a new and better civilization. The town had caught the inspiration of the whistle of the approaching locomotive, and was preparing to take its place among the cities of the Golden State as the queen of them all, in point of beauty of location and salubrity of climate.

If the reader will examine the map of California, he will find the trend of the Coast at this point almost due west, for a distance of about fifty miles, to Point Conception. The cold northern trade winds that sweep the Coast during the summer months are broken at this point, and, by the time they reach Santa Barbara, are softened into gentle breezes, with just enough of the fresh breath of the sea to make the air a delightful solace to all weak lungs.

The town is located upon an undulating plateau at the base of the Santa Inez Mountains, embracing the horseshoe-shaped Bay of Santa Barbara, and in natural advantages is really one of the most picturesque and beautiful cities in the world. Its present population is about 6000, to be doubled, doubtless, within the next five years. From its then lack of railroad communication with the outer world, it had hitherto been heavily handicapped in its race for fame; but that objection has now been removed, and we may reasonably expect to see Santa Barbara speedily rise to the importance which her beauty of location and salubrity of climate justly entitle her.

We see here, everywhere, the footprints of that grand soul and brave Spiritualist, Colonel Hollister, who lately passed on to the other life. The Arlington Hotel, one of the best caravansaries in the State, was the creation of his brain, together with many other public and private buildings. He had unbounded faith in the future of Santa Barbara, and zealously planned to that end. His dreams were just coming to be waking realities when the summons came that called him hence. But he has lost none of his interest in the town, or in his old friends, as he comes back frequently to assure us.

We arrived in Santa Barbara, on Saturday evening, where we were most cordially received by expectant friends. On Sunday evening Mr. Evans gave his usual seance to reporters, and with his usual success. The papers here are largely under the thrall of an unjust public opinion concerning Spiritualism ; hence their editors find it difficult to state a simple fact favoring our phenomena, without intruding a sneer or quibbling over the matter of the communications received. The *Press*, after describing the reporters' seance quite fairly, adds the following:

The visitors were all skeptics before the seance, are so still, and will no doubt always remain so, but unanimously decided that there was something very remarkable about this slate-writing business. The test was about all that could be desired by those present, but if any good can result from these communications, not one of this number was able to discover it.

Thus, " not one of this number " was able to discover any good result in the demonstration of the existence of an independent intelligent force in nature—a force capable of producing intelligible messages from the so-called dead to the living, within closed slates, without the touch of mortal hands! Had these reporters lived in a past age they would, doubtless, have been unable to "discover" that any good could result from believing the world was round instead of flat; or that Sir Isaac Newton, or Copernicus, or Professor Morse, were anything more than cranks when they demonstrated to the world certain great facts of nature. The conservatism that would belittle or ignore a truth of any kind, because of its unpopularity, is the conservatism of cowardice. It is what the world's great reformers and discoverers have always had to contend with. It sat on the banks of the Hudson, in Fulton's day, and sneered at his "folly" of attempting to propel a vessel by steam; it ridiculed Columbus in his proposed voyage of discovery—in short, it has "made faces" at the prophets and seers in all ages of the world, and will probably continue to do so until humanity ascends to higher levels.

After the reporters' seance, on Sunday evening, which was held at an early hour, the writer addressed an intelligent audience, at Lobero's Theatre, on the "Claims and Mission of Spiritualism," and at the same place, on Tuesday evening, Mr. Evans gave a public seance, which was an unusually fine success. There was none of the hoodlum element present which we encountered in San Diego and Los Angeles. The audience was composed of the best people of the town, orderly and passive, thus giving the medium the best possible conditions. The committee consisted of Messrs. Porter and Noble and Mrs. Iverson—all skeptics, but honest and fair-minded people. Five slates full of messages were obtained, including a likeness of the late James Brownell Clark, of Oakland. Had the wishes of Mr. Evans or of the writer been complied with, we should have had a likeness of Colonel Hollister, as we were both desirous of obtaining a picture of our old friend; but the spirit guides are the sole masters of the situation, and they give us what they will. Spirit John Gray gave the test of writing upon a slate upon which a cross had previously been made, in plain sight of the audience and committee, the slate being placed under the foot of one of the committee. The writing appeared in twelve different colors or shades. Of the numerous messages received, the following, from Colonel Hollister, was so characteristic of the writer thereof as to be readily recognized by the audience present ere the reading was one-half finished:

DEAR FRIENDS:—I am glad that this opportunity has been given me to write a few lines to my many friends here. I know there are many things left undone that I might have straightened out. But you know none of us are perfect. But I am glad to say that I am happy here in the spirit world; and though I left things a little mixed upon earth, I found everything as straight as a string in the spirit world. I am glad to predict to my many old friends that the good time that they have long looked for will soon come to pass, and dear old Santa Barbara will take the lead of California. This is what I have long looked forward to; and I will rejoice with you in the spirit world as though I were in Santa Barbara. But before this comes to pass you will have a little trouble with your railroad, which will soon be overcome, then prosperity to Santa Barbara. Give my love to my dear wife, sons, and my daughter. Tell them there are many things I regret, but let the past be buried. My old friends, Barker, Barber, Winchester, Morris, Benn, Maxwell, Owen, and many others, you all have the best wishes of W. W. Hollister. Good-night.

The message by Spirit John Gray, written in twelve colors upon the under side of a slate placed upon the floor, and under the feet of one of the committee, is also worth producing:

MY DEAR FRIENDS OF SANTA BARBARA:—I am much pleased to see you all gathered here this evening. Some of you have come here out of pure curiosity, some to investigate, whilst others come already satisfied of the truth. But you are all interested in knowing of a future life—and this is the mission of spirit return—and are eagerly awaiting a message from the spirit world. And this is the mission of the medium and Mr. Owen, to present such proof as I will, from time to time, demonstrate through them, and it remains for you to accept or reject as you will. If you accept you will find it to your own happiness and peace of mind. I will bring the medium here again soon. Until then, good-night. From spirit guide, JOHN GRAY.

Mr. Noble, of the committee, reported that, to use his own words, "there was not a scintilla of an attempt at deception practiced by the medium"—that everything was fair and above board, and that the writing was produced in some manner unknown to himself. The two other members of the committee confirmed Mr. Noble in his report.

In all of the places we have visited, Mr. Evans gave all the private sittings he was able to, the sitters almost invariably bringing their own slates, and in no instance failing to obtain messages from their spirit friends within. Scores of applicants for seances were necessarily turned away for want of time.

MR. AND MRS. EVANS IN STOCKTON.

THE following account of an interesting seance in Stockton was furnished to the *Golden Gate* by a correspondent who was present :

EDITOR OF *Golden Gate*:—Stockton is a peculiar place, made up largely of peculiar people, but since you sent your best and brightest on a sort of missionary visit here, to commemorate the Fortieth Anniversary of the dawn of Modern Spiritualism, I would like to tell you that his coming among us has sown seed which will bear abundantly, inasmuch as it has set all classes and phases of our society to *thinking*.

Fred Evans, the slate-writer, seen and heard from afar ; Fred Evans, whose modest advertisement has for months been a feature of the *Golden Gate*, and whose marvelous and almost incredible slate-writings and profile-pictures caused such food for research and speculation to your readers; and Fred Evans revealed in the full, broad light, standing on the stage of the Avon Theatre, before a critical and intelligent audience, though one and the same being, wrought a marked change in spiritualistic circles.

People are dumfounded in the face of such proof of spirit return, and while those who know as much as can be known of its truth rejoice in the beauty and comfort of these revelations, the doubters and investigators, unwilling to give up, refuse to believe the evidence of their own eyes, and say, " Oh, well, the slates you held in your hands were *changed*, but you did not know it."

Stockton has always been dubbed "the crazy town," but none of us who know of and have accepted the beautiful religion of Spiritualism but are sane enough to recognize messages and tokens of love which the heart has often ached to receive from lips which have been stilled forever on this side of the river of life.

Save a few who have advanced a long way in the new light, we are a very skeptical people as a class, but the fact of Mr. Evans' presence here induced people to visit him whose testimony would be a criticism of his ability as a medium; hence, when the evening of his public appearance arrived, the theatre was early filled with a large and intelligent audience.

Mrs. Evans gave some remarkable tests, announcing the presence of many spirits who had been attracted by the cords of love which still bound them to earth, and in many cases the spirits were recognized and acknowledged. But it was evident that slate-writing was the magnet which attracted the audience, and when Mr. Evans appeared a general air of satisfaction was noticeable upon the countenances of those present.

With brief remarks, he proposed that, as a matter of satisfaction to themselves, some member of the audience nominate a gentleman and lady to go on the stage as a committee, to see that everything was done on the square. Accordingly, Mr. James C. Gage, a noted skeptic, and Mrs. Virginia W. Bucroft were chosen. A small pine table was placed near the footlights, and upon this a tiny box with pencils, etc.; and upon a chair six small slates, which were scratched over with a slate pencil, washed off with a sponge, and rubbed dry with a white handkerchief, the slate being held up before the audience all the time during the operation.

Then two of the slates were strapped together with a broad rubber band, and given, one to Mr. Gage, and the other to the lady. The two other slates were tossed upon the floor, thus disposing of the six slates. Some ten minutes elapsed, when Mr. Colnon, of the *Mail*, was requested to come to the platform and open the slates. The gentleman quickly responded. Taking the slates from the hands of Mrs. Bucroft, he told the audience that he found closely written thereon "some twenty different messages, some in bright colors, and others in pencil, each one of which was divided by white lines, and a small portrait in one corner."

Mr. Gage's slates were found to contain a like number of messages, each one of which was a greeting to some person in the audience. These strange telegrams, on being read aloud, were recognized, and doubtless brought joy and consolation to long lonely and bereaved hearts.

On the next day, Monday, the slates were neatly framed and hung on a bulletin board on Main Street, where all day long crowds were gazing at the strange and unexplainable calligraphy.

Mr. Evans has returned to you again, but with his name and presence are associated the most astounding experiences ever met with either in public or private seances among us. He says he may come again soon, and hoping that he will find time and inclination to do so, that the good people here may have further proof of spirit return, I subscribe myself

Yours fraternally,

STOCKTON, CAL. B. W.

A "MAIL" SKEPTIC DISARMED.

Both the editor and reporter of the *Stockton Mail* called upon Mr. Evans at his rooms, and thus relate their experience :

The *Mail's* anti-Spiritualism reporter has seen a good many alleged manifestations by spirits, but they were all such transparent frauds that his unbelief was made stronger than ever—not quite all, either, for there was one medium who performed certain tricks which the reporter could not fathom; but he was caught up so many times in the seance, and fell into so many little traps laid for him, that the interviewer regarded his performance as all of a piece throughout. The readers of the *Mail* have had reports by the anti-Spiritism man from time to time, the articles on sittings, slate-writings, lectures and circles, (except that published last Monday) having been written by him.

It was, therefore, with a foregone conclusion that he would discover another fraud, that the reporter took a " detail " yesterday, and accompanied by a friend named Farnoll, rapped at the door of No. 81 in the Yo Semite house, and called for Medium Fred Evans. A young man wearing a love of a smoking-jacket responded. He had made an engagement for four o'clock, he said, and as it lacked but a few minutes of that hour, the visitors would have to wait awhile; if the party of the second part to the engagement did not show up, the interviewers would be accommodated with a sitting. During a fifteen minutes general chat which followed, the reporter studied Mr. Evans' face. The medium is apparently an Englishman, about twenty-five years old, rather dark-complexioned, and has a pleasing expression and a kind, frank manner. He is somewhat good-looking and has features indicative of a noble spirit—in other words, he looks like a newspaper reporter.

After it had become apparent that the former engagement was not to be kept, Mr. Evans invited the two visitors into his seance-room. They took seats at one side of a writing desk, Mr. Farnoll occupying a chair near a corner of it, and the medium sat at the opposite side. The reporter produced two small slates which he had just bought, and, as he thought they might perhaps leave his hands, sealed them together with slips of paper on which some name had been printed to his order. He argued that as the medium could not have duplicates of the slips, it would be impossible to open the seals without detection, even should the slates be taken into another room. The precaution, however, proved to be needless, for the slates did not leave his hands.

This test was not very satisfactory. When the slates were opened by the interviewer, at the close of the sitting, no writing was found within. There was, however, a rude profile sketch of a face, about as large as the half of a silver dollar piece. During the conversation before the sitting, Mr. Evans had said that he could not assure his visitors of the success of the sealed slate-test which they proposed; and that, as they were newspaper representatives, he did not care to undertake it, for a failure would be interpreted as a negative evidence of fraud on his part. But, on being informed that they desired that particular test, he assented.

While the reporter held the pair of slates Mr. Evans picked up two five-cent school slates, wiped them clean with a sponge, exhibited both sides of each, and handed them to Farnoll. The reporter watched this proceeding carefully to be sure that neither of the slates went below the table, for in that case it would have been an easy matter to substitute for it one that had already been written upon. But the slates were held a foot above the table—or writing desk—and were exhibited on both sides at the instant they were handed to Farnoll. He held them in his hands twenty minutes or so, and upon opening them found a closely-written message, covering one side, signed by a dead relative.

During the twenty minutes that the last-described manifestation was being awaited, the medium performed another test. He cleaned a slate, displayed both sides, and laid it down on the carpet at Mr. Farnoll's feet. In doing so, it passed for an instant behind a corner of the desk, so that this test in itself might not be considered at all satisfactory (inasmuch as there was a slight chance for substitution of slates), were it not for the other instances in which the slates were held above the table and in which there was not a ghost of a show for fraud. Farnoll placed one foot upon the slate, and after a few minutes picked the tablet up and found upon it a message from an aunt of his who died in the East, and whose name had never been mentioned by him, even in his family.

In the *interim* from time to time, while awaiting messages on the slates, Mr. Evans gave some remarkable performances. To the reporter he said a spirit was present giving a name which he could not catch exactly. He repeated three or four names, all similar to the reporter's but not identical with it. The reporter said he knew of no such person. Taking a slip of paper, the interviewer then wrote two names, folded them up, and placed them on his sealed slates. There was a bureau and its mirror at one end of the table, and, although the medium sat with his back to it and his side to the writer, the latter thought it best to avoid any possible reflection, by shading the paper from observation with his hand while he wrote. As soon as the names had been written and held beneath his thumbs on the slate, Mr. Evans remarked that he could then give the name which he had been unable to pronounce exactly before, and he spoke it. It was one of the names on the slip. He next wrote that cognomen in full, together with the spirit's two Christian names. The second name on the slip was also given.

A like manifestation was given to Mr. Farnoll. The signatures of the messages which he received were the names he had written on a billet of paper which he held in his hand.

But the last test was the most striking of all. Mr. Evans picked up a slate from the corner of the table, and remarking that the reporter might be so skeptical as to think that there was a message already written upon it, and that it was simply concealed from his sight by some wonderful chemical process, he scratched both sides of it pretty well with his pencil, spat on it, and rubbed the marks out. He then held it near the reporter's face and turned both sides of it to prove that they were clean. He next placed the slate down on the centre of the desk, with a bit of pencil under it. The reporter laid his hand upon the slate for a few moments—five or ten seconds—and then picked it up. He found upon it a message directed to himself and signed by a dead relative.

This closed the seance.

Another *Mail* man visited Mr. Evans before the performance described in the foregoing had been given. The manifestations he received were somewhat similar, but in two instances there were exceptional differences. A clean slate was laid on the carpet, and upon being picked up a message was found on it written in various colors, one running into another. The medium pointed out the fact that they were the colors of the carpet where the slate had been laid. He then cleaned a slate and with his pencil drew two diagonal lines across one side. The slate was tossed on the carpet with that side down. The interviewer took it up a few minutes afterwards and found another message in colors upon it; and an examination showed that the writing was over the diagonal lines.

This interviewer secured, also, an instantaneous message, closely written, covering the whole side of one of the slates.

"Well," queried Medium Evans, at the conclusion of the sitting, "what do you think now?"

"I think it is genuine," was the honest response.

"I'm sorry you couldn't get a message on your sealed slates, but may be you'll be more successful next time."

"Oh, it wouldn't have been a bit more conclusive, if I had."

"No, I don't think so myself; but you know a good many people won't be satisfied unless they get just what they are looking for, no matter if another is just as conclusive or not. It's a hard thing to make people believe in mediums."

"I don't blame them, judging from my own experience; no sensible man could see the average manifestations without tumbling to the tricks. You are the first and the only one who has offered convincing proof of the truth of Spiritualism, or 'odic' force, or any other unknown power that you might call it."

The Stockton *Press*, with other notices of Mr. Evans, relates the following:

* * * At another interview which a member of the management of this paper had with Mr. Fred Evans, prior to the above account, two slates were written full with messages from the father and long deceased sister of the gentleman, and then laying a slate upon the carpet, Mr. Evans said, "I think they will give you a message written in colors; put your foot upon the slate." When the slate was lifted from the floor it contained a letter written by a brother Andrew, in the same colors, line for line, as were seen in the carpet. There were no colored pencils to produce such an effect, and if, as some claim, it is chemicals on the slate, the mixture which produced one shade would destroy the other. No hand touched it while it lay there. If it was not spirit power, pray what is it? Let some of the wise ones enlighten us on the subject.

These pictures and slates can be seen at this office by anyone who thinks he can explain the mystery and tell what the power is that produces the writing on the slates that no human hand touches as they lay upon the floor, and why are lead pencil lines and portraits on the paper, and a message written with a slate pencil upon the slate, at the same time, while the paper is strapped within the two slates? If it is not spirit power, what is it? Let those who can, explain.

STANLEY ST. CLAIR.

IT was while experimenting in psychographic writing with Spirit John Gray, that Spirit Stanley St. Clair introduced himself to us, and gave us as his first experiment a good likeness of D. D. Home, the correct autograph appended thereto being given, as Mr. Gray informed us, by Mr. Home himself.

Spirit St. Clair, in his note upon the slate, says that he has given his picture as he appeared on earth, thinking some of his New Orleans friends may recognize him.

It is a singular circumstance, in these pictures, that the psychic's guide utilizes the margins of the slates for messages from himself and from other spirits. Thus, upon the slate we present herewith, the reader will note the words, "See that hand is worked right, Mr. O." That refers to an experimental seance mentioned elsewhere, wherein, while sitting in the dark with the psychic's hands joined with ours, a luminous spirit hand manipulated the pencils within the slates in our hands. We said to the guide (John Gray) at the time, that we should endeavor to have the incident illustrated for our paper. He now, a week later, charges us to see that the hand "is worked right."

In our experiments with Mr. Evans on one occasion, we were informed by John Gray that we should have no picture at that time, as St. Clair was not present—"but," he said, "I have seen how he does it, and if you wish, Mr. Owen, I will try and sketch your portrait." "All right," we replied, and in a few minutes he produced, upon a slate under our hands, a rough sketch that could be readily recognized. It was patterned after St. Clair's pictures, but the work was much inferior. "How is that," he wrote under the picture, "for a first attempt?"

These sketches, as we have frequently stated, are given independently, through the mediumship of Fred Evans, in the full light, upon slates held in our own hands, and upon which we *know positively* there was no previous preparation, picture or writing of any kind. The writer's wife is generally, but not always, present at these experimental seances, and *knows*, as do we, that they are the production of an independent, intelligent occult power.

It will be seen that, upon the margin of the slate containing the likeness of the artist, it is written that the next picture would be the likeness of the psychic's well-known control, Spirit John Gray, for the appearance of which many of his friends are anxiously looking.

The time was appointed by the artist for this seance, a fact which we incidentally mentioned to a few persons who are deeply interested in these experiments. We were on hand as per appointment, when it was written upon the slates, over the signature of St. Clair, that so many minds were centered upon the experiment for that evening that it would seriously interfere with the work, and that he would be obliged to defer the attempt for a day or two, whereof he would advise us. John Gray also added a few lines in which he facetiously expressed his disappointment at not obtaining the likeness.

We then asked St. Clair several questions concerning his history, which were promptly answered by telegraphic raps upon the table. He stated in reply to our questions, that he "passed on" from New Orleans fifteen years ago; that he had no studio there, his work being mostly of a private character; that during the war he was a resident of Germany, studying his art; that there were persons residing in New Orleans who would remember him; that he remembered the lady in Oakland who had known him and recognized his likeness as published in the *Golden Gate*, etc. We then asked him if he could not vary the programme and give us some other picture a landscape sketch, or something that the mental influence of others, to which he had referred, would not affect. He said, if we had time to wait, he would try.

Mr. Evans then took two large slates, both of which were thoroughly cleaned and placed upon the table under our hands. After about fifteen minutes, a signal from the artist announced the completion of the work, when upon one of the slates was found what St. Clair called a rough sketch, in colors, of a portion of the old German town where he had resided for a number of years. The green of the foliage, the blue of the water, the background of pine forest, and the red roof tiles, are all there, constituting the most marvelous production by independent spirit power we have yet witnessed. In the foreground of the picture is a wolf, and the artist informed us that the wolves were quite numerous there, and were frequently seen in the streets of the town where he resided.

On the following day we received a note from Mr. Evans, stating that if we would call at his residence then, the artist would give us the promised picture of his psychographic control, as no minds were fixed upon the subject then to interfere with his work. We called at about midday, and upon preparing the slates as usual, the picture, as it appears, was produced. The time occupied in its production was not to exceed one minute, and the entire seance scarcely lasted five minutes.

St. Clair informed us, on one occasion, that he was experimenting with a process whereby he hoped to be able to produce permanent pictures of mortals and spirits upon slates.

At our next seance for experimental work through Mr. Evans, the wife of the writer was present. At this seance we obtained twelve slates full of messages and pictures, including some very interesting work by St. Clair's new process. The artist was delighted with the result, and says that he will be able to excel, by this process, all of his former efforts in spirit picture making.

OUR SPIRIT ARTIST.

[Sketched by himself, independently, through the mediumship of Fred' Evans, upon the inner surface of one of a pair of slates held in the hands of Mr. and Mrs. J. J. Owen.]

Upon the under surface of two slates placed upon the table, which we first held singly, edgewise, between our hands, and which never for a moment left our hands or sight, a number of pictures were produced, which seem to be as permanent as the material upon which they appear. A space some four inches square in the centre of each slate has been subjected to some glazing process, *in* which glazing, not upon its surface, the pictures appear to be photographed. Upon one slate there are four faces, and upon the other, three. Two of the pictures on each slate are good likenesses of the writer and Mrs. Owen. Then appear two spirit faces, one of which is that of John Gray, and the other, which is quite dim, is given as a spirit sister of Mrs. Owen. Around the edges of the glazed surfaces is a number of private messages, thirteen in all, given mainly in close imitation of the writing of the persons from whom they purport to come.

Upon nine of the slates is a private letter to us, running continuously from one slate to another, from John Gray. He seemed to be in the humor for a friendly chat. Speaking of St. Clair's work upon the slates, he says: "You remember some eighteen months ago, he promised to give you pictures on slates prepared with some kind of paint or varnish. Well, we have just made the second experiment, and find that we shall soon improve on it. The slate is first sensitized by some process known to St. Clair, and then the intended pictures are photographed on. Mortals can have their pictures taken along side of their spirit friends, just the same as you have received to-night. We can have your face reflected on the clouds, have your spirit friends near it, and photograph them both." It is certainly very remarkable.

TESTS BY PROXY.

JIM G. ANDERSON, as he always wrote his name, late editor of the Richmond (Mo.) *Democrat*, now passed over to spirit life, wrote to the author, enclosing a lock of his hair, and asked that we represent him—in a sitting with Mr. Evans—in an endeavor to procure some messages from his spirit friends. No names were given, of course, nor ballots enclosed. He was entirely unknown to us, save that he had written us once before asking for an exchange of papers. Accompanied by Mrs. Owen, we took the letter to Mr. Evans, and placed it upon a pair of slates with our four hands resting thereon, Mr. Evans sitting upon the opposite side of the table with his hands unoccupied. Other slates were placed upon the table, and one or two upon the floor. Four of the slates were written full. There were five or six messages, all signed by names unknown to us. One of the messages purported to come from the spirit father of Mr. Anderson.

We forwarded these slates to Mr. Anderson, and in due time received the following reply:

RICHMOND, Mo., June 24, 1886.

DEAR BROTHER OWEN:—The slates have just arrived. In spite of the excellent manner in which you packed them the slate on which the colored writing was done was broken. By pasting board on the back I have it all O. K. save a little sliver off one side. The writing can readily be read on this and all the slates. * * * The test is in the message signed C. P. Anderson, the signature being as near that of my father as can be. His writing was peculiar. It is so pronounced that my foreman, who worked with me when my father did in 1879-80, recognized the signature at once. The names Mary and Elizabeth are my sisters, but neither George Anderson nor J. Anderson is known, any more than I have a cousin and an uncle whose first name was J. or John. (Pshaw! It comes to me as I write that it is my cousin Jim T. Anderson, who was accidentally killed over a year ago.) My mother may be able to place George Anderson. I knew of a prominent man of that name but did not know him intimately. The message from my father is enough as a test, and I consider the result astonishing under the circumstances. It is the best I ever heard of by proxy. May the angels bless you.

Fraternally,   JIM G. ANDERSON.

Thus was the proof to us absolutely conclusive of spirit existence, as it must have been to him. But now our friend has solved the problem for himself, and knows of a verity that there is no death.

His successor on the paper speaks of Mr. Anderson as follows:

On account of his peculiar views in regard to the hereafter, Mr. Anderson had many heated controversies, and yet throughout them all he demeaned himself as a gentleman should, never once descending to degrading personalities. His was always a warfare in the open field and never from ambush. He was a firm believer in the doctrine of spirit communion, and who can say he was wrong? He had what he considered indisputable evidence that the spirits of departed loved ones can and do communicate with the living, and was earnest and honest in the belief. He died in the belief that one day his spirit would return to cheer his grief-stricken companion and aged and bedridden mother.

The "indisputable evidence" alluded to was doubtless that furnished him by the crucial tests above mentioned.

SPIRIT CAMELIA.

ANOTHER picture produced independently by Stanley St. Clair, was that of Spirit Camelia.
This remarkable picture was produced in presence of the writer and wife. It was produced upon the under surface of a single slate lying upon the table, under Mrs. Owen's hands, in full gaslight, and without contact of the hands of any other person; time, less than two minutes.

On the inner surfaces of two other slates held by the writer at the same time, was a message from the psychic's guide, John Gray, in which he says: "The picture that St. Clair has given you this evening I want to go in this week's *Golden Gate*. This spirit's name is Camelia. She will play an important part in our intended spiritual mission. We will give you her history and the work she will do for you soon." We cheerfully complied with his request.

The message concluded as follows: "I will let you know about that motor in a few days, when I see the engineers."

In calling upon Mr. and Mrs. Evans on that evening we had no intention of sitting for experimental work, our object being simply a friendly call, except that we wished to submit to the guide an ingenious device for a wave motor, in the success of which we had, or thought we might possibly have in the future, a vicarious and remotely contingent interest, with the request that he obtain the opinion of some good spirit engineers thereon, as to its practical working. (This he promised to do and has since done.)

St. Clair informed us that he was preparing something of far greater merit than anything he had yet produced, whereof we should be advised hereafter.

These intelligences, John Gray and Stanley St. Clair,

SPIRIT CAMELIA.
[Taken independently, through the mediumship of Fred Evans.]

are veritable entities to us. Our intercourse with them is of the most friendly and pleasing character. They are ever ready to answer our questions, which they do by telegraphic raps and also by direct writing. They are both able and faithful workers for the enlightenment of humanity.

Referring to the picture of Camelia, whom the guide stated had come to the psychic's band for the purpose of introducing a negative element, which would increase the power of the controlling spirit to overcome strong positive conditions in the presence of investigators, she promised at some future time to give us a history of her life, which we herewith present, as written independently, between closed slates.

Brother L. L. Whitlock, editor of *The Soul* magazine, of Boston, had written to us, requesting that we represent him in a seance with Mr. Evans. So, on the evening named, we called on Mr. Evans for that purpose, and also to have a little chat with his spirit manager, John Gray, and such other friends as might happen to be present. Now, we hadn't the slightest knowledge of Brother Whitlock's spirit friends, except of some of those who are the common property of humanity. His kindred are wholly unknown to us, as we doubt not they are to Mr. Evans; and yet, under our own hands and eyes, upon two slates that we *know* were thoroughly clean, there were placed, in a few minutes' time, seventeen messages, in as many different styles of writing, one of which, of eleven lines, was written in eleven different shades of color. There was also one fine picture of a young Indian girl in colors, and two small pencil heads. Some of the messages are written so fine that they can be read only by the aid of a magnifier.

The under surfaces of four other slates were written full, under the same test conditions—two from John Gray containing a private message to us, and two others—very large ones—containing the following message from Camelia:

SPIRIT CAMELIA.

DEAR FRIEND OF THE EARTH PLANE:—By the request of Spirit John Gray, and with the assistance of other kind spirits, I am enabled to give you a brief history of my life when on earth, and my transition to the spirit world, also my attraction to this medium and his work.

My earthly name was Kleoptra. I was born in Rome, in the year 1790. My parents were of a noble family, but, through strange manifestations occurring in our family, we were shunned and abandoned by all our friends. The priests claimed that some member of our household was possessed of the Evil One, and if we could discover which was possessed and cast him out-doors, the rest of the family would be free from contamination. I was then seventeen years old. The priest suggested that all should leave the house, so that he could banish the supposed Evil One. But being frightened, he abandoned that idea, and asked that we should again enter the house, and that I should sit near him, when suddenly the table that was between us came along side me, and many startling manifestations did occur that caused the priest to declare that I was possessed of the Evil One and should die. My father then, with fear and trembling, smote me on the head with a toul, [The spirit stated afterward, in answer to a question, that a "toul" was a kind of spiked club of small size.—THE AUTHOR.] and my spirit left my body in 1807.

I have often visited many friends on earth since I left the body, and as I generally show myself to them as I appeared when on earth, I always come with a white camellia to hide the mark of the cruel blow my father struck me through ignorance of spiritual laws, for, as you will see by the above narrative, I was being used as a medium by some departed friend when our priest charged me with being obsessed with the Evil One.

I became interested in this medium's welfare when I found him giving public exhibitions before large critical audiences. I could see that certain elements were lacking to make the presentation of this phenomenon a comparatively easy one. The medium's only two guides are males, or positive elements, whilst the committee picked to examine the *modus operandi* of the writing are always male positives of the most pronounced type, thus making a complete positive element to overcome. In one of your public meetings I determined to introduce a female or negative element, and you know well the results. The production of the writing was made easy, and all by placing a negative between two positives. This caused me to come to the conclusion that I could become of great use to the medium and the cause he demonstrates by becoming the negative guide between the two positive guides, John Gray and Stanley St. Clair.

I will at an early date give you, in detail, the manner of the production of independent slate-writing, independent pictures, and other demonstrations that have occurred through this medium, Fred Evans, and which has interested you and so many readers of your paper. * * * We have been working spiritually with this medium to prepare him for work that will bring him prominently before the world. With kind regards to you and your partner in life, believe me to remain your friend, and one of the medium's guides,

CAMELIA.

On spreading these six slates out upon the table we were struck with the large amount of writing and drawing that had been done in so short a time—not exceeding twenty minutes—and we expressed the wish that John Gray would give us the number of words upon each slate. He did so without a moment's hesitation, naming the number upon each slate, and then giving the total as 1,582, and in less time than it has taken us to write this sentence. We afterwards counted the words upon two of these slates and found the number to correspond with that given by the spirit.

Can any one explain the system of computation whereby such marvelous results are obtained? It evidently shows a power of comprehension to which we mortals are strangers, although there are a few instances on record—as in the case of the "Lightning Calculator"—where similar powers have been manifested by mortals.

Truly the field opens and the vision broadens, as we explore the realm of spiritual things.

AN INTERESTING EXPERIMENT.

[From *The Soul*, Boston, February, 1888.]

FOR a long time we have been very much interested in the account of independent drawings and writings that have been published in the *Golden Gate*, of San Francisco, Cal. These have shown great spirit power

through the fine powers of Mr. Fred Evans, and enterprise and ability to receive on the part of our esteemed friend and co-laborer, Mr. J. J. Owen, the editor of the above-named valuable journal.

Some weeks ago we asked Mr. Owen if he would conduct a seance with Mr. Evans for *The Soul*. The following letter sufficiently explains:—

SAN FRANCISCO, CAL., December 23, 1887.

BROTHER WHITLOCK :—In response to your request, I represented you with Fred Evans last evening, and obtained for you two very nice slates—with picture, colored writing, and some seventeen messages. I see several of your name, but whether the Christian names are correct or not neither Mr. Evans nor myself has any means of knowing. I *know* that whatever appears upon the slates was put there by an occult power. The slates were thoroughly cleansed, and from first to last were under my own hands and sight. I obtained in addition four slates for myself, mostly of a private character, but of which I shall speak in my next issue. Should you have either of the slates engraved for *The Soul*, please send me an electrotype for the *Golden Gate*. You will see that "Johnny" gives me credit for the force that enabled him to produce such fine results. I do not think I deserve it, although I think he can do better with than without me. Fraternally yours, J. J. OWEN.

Our illustration, without the colors, shows imperfectly the picture drawn upon the slates. The flesh tint is as perfect as possible, and the dress is in several colors. We do not recognize the Indian maiden, but hope she will in some way identify herself.

H. Whitlock is a brother who passed to spirit life about forty years ago, when a small child. We occasionally hear from him, and believe he could not have been known to any person present. The others of our name, especially father and sister, are recognized.

SLATE ILLUSTRATED.

The spirit of Owaseka is here, and sends love to his medium, Squaw Whitlock.

I have come by request to write a few lines for you, to tender you my best wishes for your future success, and to promise you my every aid. I am always pleased to add another item to the truth of spirit return. BENJAMIN RUSH.

I am here, and will soon come to you at your home and manifest there. From
BROTHER ROBERT.

You have my best wishes in your endeavor to publish to the world the "facts" of spiritual phenomena, for it will appeal to the "souls" of all beings who aspire to better their future and to know of an immortal future. This from WILLIAM DENTON.

MY DEAR OLD FRIEND:—I am going to give you my every aid to further your work for the advancement of spiritual phenomena, and make the prediction that you will change the form of your magazine in the future to one of more importance, and will be satisfied of the result of your work in a few months. JUDGE EDMOND.

I have come to bear my testimony to the truth of spirit return. ROBERT HARE, M. D.

Baby Helen is here. Also Charles and H.

I am with you in spirit, but absent in body. JAMES.

The spirit of St. Clair has given this as an exhibition of his work. ST. CLAIR.

FRIEND WHITLOCK:—At the request of our medium, Fred Evans, we have brought together numerous spirits, who have kindly given their best assistance for the production of this slate for the benefit of *The Soul*. We must thank J. J. Owen, editor of the *Golden Gate*, for acting as proxy for you, and thus furnishing the necessary forces for the production of this slate.
JOHN GRAY.

SECOND SLATE.

I have come to give you these few lines as a test of spirit power. This from the spirit of
H. WHITLOCK.

[This message was written in eleven colors.—ED.]

MY DEAR SON LEWIS:—It is with pleasure that I respond to the medium's invitation, given to me and other spirit friends, to come and write a few lines to you, although it is difficult for us to come through a strange medium without you or any other member of our family to attract us; yet we have succeeded in establishing the fact that spirits can and do operate without the well-worn plea of *mind-reading*, and that we can communicate without the presence of our friends, and, under conditions that need an independent, intelligent force, aside from the medium or sitter, write other messages to you through this medium in the near future. Give my kind love to all the folks at home, and believe me to remain the happy spirit of your loving father, GEORGE CLINTON WHITLOCK.

I am with you in spirit, and am pleased to write these few lines to you.
E. WHITLOCK.

MY DEAR BROTHER LEWIS:—I am much pleased to be able to write a few lines for you. We will have more to say to you soon through this medium, and will soon give you information that will assist you to carry out your work to better advantage. Give my love to your wife and mother, also to my niece, who will soon make a good medium. This from your loving sister, SARAH WHITLOCK.

I am glad to come back and prove to you that I still live. HOWARD HENRY.

The spirit of John Gray is here, and he sends best wishes to Mr. I. L. Whitlock.
JOHN GRAY.

SPIRIT JOHN GRAY.

[A brief sketch of his life written by himself, independently, within closed slates.]

I WAS born in London, England, June 10, 1816, and commenced a seafaring life in December, 1830. After making many voyages and experiencing two shipwrecks, I returned to London in 1835. I then began to experience strange visitations, which, of course, I know now to have been from the spirit world, and who advised me to ship at once for America. So on the seventeenth of August, 1835, I shipped on the ship "Chevey Chase," bound for New York, under the command of Captain Roberts. August 30th found us leaving West End Dock for New York, at which place we arrived December 25, 1835. I secretly left the vessel on its arrival, and kept away until she left New York homeward bound. I then applied for and was received as Coast Guardsman.

My duties often gave me time and opportunity to converse with my (then) invisible spirit friends, who used to rap on the rocks on the beach during my patrol, in answer to my questions of inquiry, often foretelling events that were to happen, such as shipwrecks, seizures, etc.; and I in turn would warn my mates, until they began to regard me as the Evil One when they saw these prophecies fulfilled.

John King often materialized for me when going my nightly rounds on the beach, and told me I had not long to stay on the earth plane, but had a great work to do in the spirit world. His prophecy came to pass October 27, 1837, when the bark "Espray" was wrecked off the coast, and in attempting to save her crew I was drowned, and thus came to the spirit world in all the health and vigor of manhood at the age of twenty-one years, four months, and seventeen days, but with the knowledge of a new home in store for me.

[This picture was taken by independent spirit power, between closed slates, in the hand of the author, the time occupied in its production being less than one minute.]

After meeting many old friends who had crossed the river before me, and who kindly assisted me to understand the workings of my new quarters, I commenced to control various mediums, moving my influence from one to another, as I found their moral, mental, and physical conditions more suited to aid me in demonstrating, beyond a doubt, the existence of spiritual beings who once inhabited the earth plane, until I found my present medium, Fred Evans, whose past life resembled my own when on earth, inasmuch as he has followed the sea and has met with many of the same experiences that I passed through. I impressed him to come to California so that I could demonstrate through him, knowing that this was a good field to spread the knowledge of spirit return.

I have found my medium best suited morally, mentally and physically, to carry out my work through him of enlightening humanity, and I hope for greater things in the near future that will enable me to place spirit phenomena before your skeptical world in such a manner as to convince the most skeptical inquirer (if he is only honest to himself) that these manifestations come from the source claimed for them.

I must now thank J. J. Owen, of the *Golden Gate*, for his honest and earnest endeavors to place before the world the *facts* and *proofs* of spirit phenomena that have come under his notice during his investigations with my medium, and also to the many spiritual and secular papers that have recounted their experiences and re-published in their columns that witnessed by their contemporaries, for they have all united in spreading this knowledge of spirit return and causing those who are in darkness to seek the light. With the happy knowledge that I will one day meet you all and welcome you to the spirit side of life, I remain your co-worker in spirit, JOHN GRAY.

REMARKABLE EXPERIENCE.

A RECEIPT CARRIED 1300 MILES BY SPIRITS.

DURING Mr. Evans' sojourn in Melbourne, the following remarkable phenomenon occurred: About eleven o'clock on the morning of April 20, 1889, Mr. Evans placed two slates together for the purpose of consulting his guide, John Gray, on some matters of importance. After the writing had ceased, Mr. Evans opened the slates and was surprised to see lying on the lower slate a printed slip with writing upon it. On examination it proved to be a receipt for an amount paid by Alexander Costello for examination on his legal qualifications for admission to the Queensland Bar. On the slate was found written the following explanatory message:

DEAR FRED:—Enclosed in these slates you will find a receipt belonging to Alexander Costello. I took it from his study in Merton Road, South Brisbane, as a test of spirit power, and I now desire you to forward the receipt to Mr. Costello, detailing the circumstances. Your guide,

JOHN GRAY.

Mr. Evans immediately forwarded the receipt and explanation to Mr. Costello, and, on April 27th, received the following letter:

MERTON ROAD, SOUTH BRISBANE, April 25, 1889.

DEAR MR. EVANS:—It was as great a surprise to me as it was to you when I opened your letter, and found the receipt for the examination fee within it. Strange that I was thinking about the paper only a few days ago, and the advisability of having it should it be wanted. Have shown your letter to Mr. Widdop (Justice of the Peace), and he requested me to ask John Gray (through you) how the phenomenon occurred. * * * I have been doing my best to think over the matter, and am inclined to think that the last time I saw the paper was in my study, *and that—since you left for Melbourne.* * * * I have no doubt whatever in my own mind that our unseen friend took the paper to Melbourne only a short time ago. * * *

Yours sincerely, ALEXANDER COSTELLO.

Here was a piece of paper, measuring about 3x6 inches—surreptitiously removed from a desk in the private room of a gentleman in Brisbane, and carried by Spirit John Gray to Melbourne and there deposited between closed slates, proving conclusively the power of spirits over matter. The distance between the place the paper was removed from and deposited in is about 1300 miles. Mr. Evans had never been in Mr. Costello's house, and had not been within 1000 miles of Brisbane for over three months and a half.

SPIRIT JOSEPHINE.

EXPERIMENTS in any phase of psychic phenomena, to be of value to the world, must be had under what is termed "test conditions." To Spiritualists, who need no such conditions—especially when sitting with psychics whom they have once tested and know to be genuine—the manifestations may be, and often are, of the most marvelous character. But while true and unquestioned by themselves, or others who are familiar with like manifestations, the recital thereof has but little, if any, weight with the skeptical world, who are ever ready to attribute our phenomena to any and everything except the true cause.

Hence it is that in our experiments and investigations in psychography, or independent slate-writing, we have ever aimed to present only such facts as we *knew* to be true. The various illustrations we have given have, with but few exceptions, been of this character.

Of this character, also, is the likeness appearing in this connection as Josephine, the beautiful spirit sister of Mrs. Mattie P. Owen. This spirit passed to the higher life about twenty-five years ago, in the bright dawn of a beautiful and useful womanhood. In her earth-life she possessed rare graces of body and mind, and is now a radiant presence among the shining ones who are our constant companions and co-workers in behalf of humanity, and in unfolding the grand truths of spirit existence.

Josephine first made her presence known to us while we were sojourning in the city of New Orleans, during the winter of 1885-'86. Seeing a notice of a psychic for independent slate-writing in one of the city papers, the writer dropped in at his rooms one day and requested a seance. We were soon convinced that the medium was a genuine psychographist, as we received messages, written independently, from two persons whom we knew well in earth-life, and in the *fac simile* of their hand-writing. The psychic then said that there was the spirit of a beautiful young lady present who wished to send a message to the wife of the writer. We asked him how he knew he had a wife. He replied that that was what he understood the spirit to say. He then placed a pair of slates in a chair some three feet distant from where we were sitting, when soon a long message appeared within, beautifully written, addressed to " My Dear Sister," and signed affectionately, " Josephine." In this message was given the name of another of Mrs. Owen's sisters in spirit-life, and also the full names of two friends of the writer. Since then Josephine has been a constant companion and friend, manifesting herself to us frequently.

The picture we present herewith was obtained at an experimental seance held with Fred Evans, the writer and his wife being the only mortals present besides the psychic. A single slate, upon which we knew there was no trace or device, was placed upon the table, with a small bit of lead, and also of slate pencil beneath. No hand touched the slate except that of Mrs. Owen. In less than five minutes raps upon the slate indicated that the work was finished.

The artist, Spirit Stanley St. Clair, then wrote upon another slate, under our own hands, saying that if we would give him a larger slate he would take another picture in a different style, and then we could judge which was the better. The slates were furnished, and in a few minutes another picture appeared, but we did not think it equal in merit to the first.

A significant fact in connection with the picture we present, is, that at a seance held in our own home on the afternoon preceding the seance with Mr. Evans, Mrs. Owen and a lady friend being the only persons present, the question was asked

Spirit Josephine

[The likeness, as she appears in spirit life, of a beautiful young sister of Mrs. Mattie P. Owen. The picture, of which the above is a copy, was taken through the mediumship of Fred Evans, in the presence of the writer, upon the under surface of a single slate placed upon a table in full light, and under Mrs. Owen's hands. Time, about five minutes.]

as to what would be the nature of the manifestations at the evening's experimental seance. The answer was spelled out that a likeness of Josephine would be given. This fact was carefully withheld from Mr. Evans.

No mere wood engraving, which only presents the lights and shades of a picture, can do the subject justice. The color of the eyes, the delicate tints of the lips and cheek, and portions of the drapery, are of course omitted. The artist invariably furnishes his own colors, and applies them with excellent taste and skill.

As to the fact of the picture being produced by independent spirit power, we simply *know* it to be true. Of course there are those who think we are the victims of deception. We can not blame them. These modern revelations of psychic power are too much for the unschooled comprehension.

At a subsequent seance with Fred Evans, we received the following communication from Josephine, written on the two inner surfaces of a pair of slates held in our own hands, explaining the symbol of the seven stars seen upon her head. [We may add that Mrs. Owen had left by steamer on the afternoon of that day for San Diego, a fact of which the psychic, until the moment of sitting, had no knowledge; hence, Josephine's reference to her departure is positive proof that there could have been no previous preparation of the slates.] The message reads as follows:

Good evening, Brother James. I see that Mattie has gone for a little trip. But you know that I am very happy to see you have come here this evening. Mr. Gray requests me to explain the meaning of the seven stars that you see in my hair represented on the picture. Well, I will tell you: I belong to a band of spirits who act as missionaries to aid and uplift the fallen and assist them to a higher sphere. The number of stars designates the zeal and development we have made in our particular work. You see I have progressed sufficiently to be awarded the seventh star. All spirits belonging to this order wear a star, so that they are recognized when manifesting anywhere. I am glad that you are both pleased with my picture. Mr. St. Clair says that he

will give you a paper proof in a little time, but not to-night. You can give my love to dear Mattie, and tell her you are going to meet with a very pleasant surprise soon. I see that you and the medium are going to do some good work in a little time, when John Gray is ready. This from loving
JOSEPHINE.

ST. CLAIR'S PICTURE OF SHAKESPEARE.

AMONG the many pictures we have obtained through Mr. Evans, that of Shakespeare, given in this connection, we regard as one of the best. That it was produced independently, through Fred Evans, on the under surface of a single slate, placed upon the table in plain sight, and under other hands than those of Mr. Evans, we do know—if we know anything. Hon. I. C. Steele, of Pescadero, President of the Grangers' Bank, San Francisco, who was also present, will bear witness to the fact here stated. It was taken at the time that Ignatius Donnelly was claiming that Bacon was the author of Shakespeare's plays.

The seance was held at the request of the writer, for the benefit of Mr. Steele. We each of us held a single slate edgewise upon the table for a few moments, between the palms of the two hands, and then placed the slates down with our hands resting thereon. Other slates were placed upon the floor. In a few minutes there appeared upon the under surface of our own slate the following message:

> Through the solicitation of John Gray I have permitted my picture to be given you, which is a correct representation of myself as I appeared when on earth. I am sorry to see that many are now debating as to the true authorship of certain works that were credited to me. I wish to mention the fact that Lord Bacon ought to be credited with an half interest in all the works attributed to me, for he was my main help and adviser in all my labors.
>
> Yours in spirit, WILLIAM SHAKESPEARE.

Upon the under surface of the slate held by Mr. Steele appeared the picture of Shakespeare, as our engraver has reproduced it, in all except the coloring (in the original the coat is a light green) and the name of the spirit artist, St. Clair, which appears upon the collar.

OCCULT ART.

[This picture was taken independently, through the mediumship of Fred Evans, under absolute test conditions, upon a slate held in the hands of Hon. I. C. Steele, of Pescadero, and in presence of the author.]

Here is a significant point which we ask the skeptical reader to notice. There are many who think that these slate pictures, together with the written messages, are prepared in advance, and that by some smart jugglery on the part of Mr. Evans, the slates are changed in our hands. Now, upon taking up the slate containing this picture of Shakespeare, we noticed that the artist had omitted the usual imprint of his name. We asked him why he had done so. He immediately replied, by telegraphic raps, that John Gray had directed us to take up the slate a little too soon—that he (the artist) was not quite ready for us. We replaced the slate, with a small bit of lead pencil under it, and the name was immediately written upon the collar, as seen in the picture!

Mr. Steele also received a fine picture of a beautiful little girl who claimed to be his niece who died in infancy. Upon another slate he received nine messages in different handwritings, and all signed with the names of nine of his spirit friends and relatives. Taking another slate and wrapping it in a pocket handkerchief, he held it aloof from the table for a few minutes, when there appeared a message upon it in some six or eight bright colors, signed by the name of a brother-in-law of Mr. Steele, Selden J. Finney.

We doubt very much if Mr. Evans is familiar with the claim set up by Ignatius Donnelly and others that Lord Bacon, and not Shakespeare, was the author of the plays attributed to the latter. If he is, it makes no difference as to the fact of the writing in the manner stated. We give the message for what it is worth. As to the picture and the manner of its production, together with the other picture and messages, we claim for them that they were produced by independent spirit power. If we do not *know* this, our three senses of sight, hearing and feeling are positively worth nothing to us.

A SPIRIT INDIAN MAIDEN.

THE spirit picture of the Indian maiden, whose name is withheld, is one of the guides of a private medium now retired from public work. The guide is bright, beautiful, vivacious, witty, and very interesting. Her utterances abound in wise sayings, for which she takes no credit to herself, but always attributes them to her teacher, who is also a guide of the same medium, and is a spirit of great intelligence.

This spirit passed to spirit-life in infancy, many years ago. She was partly of Indian parentage, her mother being a princess of her tribe. She always presents herself as a lively little maiden, full of sunshine.

The picture was taken through the mediumship of Mr. Fred Evans. It was taken in the presence of the author and his wife, and in the following manner: Three slates were first thoroughly cleaned with a damp sponge and wiped dry. One of these slates was placed upon the floor, in plain sight, and Mrs. Owen was requested by Mr. Evans to place a foot upon it, which she did. The others were under our two pair of hands upon the table, Mr. Evans sitting unconcernedly upon the opposite side of the table, and fully four feet from where the slate lay upon the floor. Subsequently, and while the work was progressing, another slate was placed upon the floor by the side of the former.

We were not really expecting a picture of this spirit at this time; in fact, the spirit artist had intimated to us the Sunday previous that it would probably be two weeks before he again attempted it. In about a quarter of an hour from the beginning of the seance the familiar raps signaled that the work was finished. On raising the slates from the floor it was found that

INDIAN MAIDEN.
[First work of Stanley St. Clair. Obtained through the mediumship of Fred Evans.]

upon the under side of the one upon which the foot rested was the picture as seen in our engraving. On the under side of the other was the following message from the artist:

To MR. OWEN—*Dear Friend:*—At the request of John Gray I take this mode of introducing myself to you, and also to our worthy medium. As you will see, I have taken the picture of the Indian maiden, ——. This spirit is of such a lively temperament as to make it extremely difficult to give a correct picture of her. But she has robed herself to her own satisfaction, and has expressed herself as being pleased with her picture, and also states that her medium will be much delighted with the results of this sitting. When I become more accustomed to the control of this medium, and with the assistance of his powerful guides, I will endeavor to give you some very good manifestations, which will reflect much credit on the medium and yourself. I have come to stay with this medium, conditions permitting. With best wishes to all, I remain yours in spirit, STANLEY ST. CLAIR.

On the under side of one of the slates upon the table was a friendly message to the writer from Mr. Evans' psychographic control, Spirit John Gray, written in his usual crisp and ready manner.

It is a significant fact that the little Indian maiden represented in the picture, wholly unknown to Mr. Evans or to us, had, on Saturday evening previous, informed her medium that the artist would sketch her likeness at our seance on the following day.

As to the fact of the messages and the picture being produced as stated, by occult or spirit power, there is not an intelligent person in the universe, with the same opportunity for observation as ourselves, who would question it for a moment.

The spirit picture of Professor Denton, like most of the pictures presented in this volume, was taken under our own hands, without the possibility of deception. In fact, it is an insult to common sense to imagine that such things can be done in the broad light of day, and under one's own eyes and hands, in any other manner than that claimed for them.

Of course no very fine work can be expected upon a slate and with the materials used. But this of Professor Denton is surely an excellent likeness and a very creditable piece of work.

The reader will understand that the background for the picture is made by whitening the surface of the slate with a bit of slate pencil, placed under a single slate upon a table, or between a pair of slates, after which the likeness is produced with a lead pencil placed in the same manner. The work is all done by the spirit artist.

The messages in the margins are doubtless from those from whom they purport to come. It will be noticed that Indian Jim, a spirit that occasionally comes to Mr. Evans, has given us a profile of his not particularly handsome face.

A somewhat striking test concerning the production of this picture is worthy of mention. While Spirit St. Clair was at work upon it, we asked Spirit John Gray what the picture was to be. He replied that the artist was complying with a wish of the wife of the writer, who was not present, and whose wishes in the matter were unknown, both to us and to Mr. Evans. "What is that?" we asked; but the spirit pleasantly evaded an answer. On meeting Mrs. Owen an hour later we inquired what wish she had entertained with regard to the expected picture. She replied that she had desired that we might obtain a likeness of Professor Denton! And there it was.

The spirit pictures which we have given in this volume, produced, as we claim, by independent spirit power, through Mr. Fred Evans, are worthy of the most serious consideration of scientists.

The pictures are all of persons who have passed to spirit life, and as they appeared in mortal life. No high art is claimed for them; and yet, as slate pencil sketches, considering the brief time and peculiar manner in which they are produced, they are certainly excellent. That this development will lead to a higher order of art, we have no doubt.

The picture of Dr. Benjamin Rush was produced upon

SPIRIT PICTURE OF PROFESSOR DENTON.

a slate which was first thoroughly washed and dried by a committee chosen by a public audience at the theatre in San Diego, on the occasion of the visit of Mr. Evans and the writer to that city. That it is a good likeness of the eminent physician, no one familiar with his features will deny.

A peculiarity of all these pictures is the utilizing of the space around the sides with private messages from the spirit world to persons present or in the neighborhood of the seance. Why this is done we are unable to say, unless it is to show that the picture was actually produced at the time and place claimed for it.

The reader will bear in mind that we have had every possible opportunity for careful and thorough investigation of Mr. Evans' psychographic powers. We regard him as the most wonderful medium in the world for this phase of spiritual phenomena. Those who would question the genuineness of these manifestations of his powers are simply ignorant of the facts.

MR. AND MRS. EVANS' TRIP TO AUSTRALIA.

THE fame of Fred Evans' mediumship had gone abroad, until the name of the medium had become familiar to investigators of psychic truth throughout the world. He was in the receipt of urgent letters of appeal to visit different parts of the country, to demonstrate the possibility of spirit return; but with very few of these letters was there any inducement for him of a financial nature, and Fred was unable to meet the heavy expense of journeys to distant parts. But not so with one letter from the Psychological Society of Brisbane, Australia. They offered to pay the expenses of himself and wife to that far-distant region, and offered other favorable inducements which prompted him to consider the matter. The fare alone from San Francisco to Brisbane was over $400 for the two, and the time required for the journey a little more than a month.

In August, 1888, the terms having been satisfactorily arranged, Mr. and Mrs. Evans sailed from San Francisco to the Australian Colonies by the steamship " Alameda," Captain Morse. The trip was a very restful and delightful one, especially to our sailor boy, Fred, whose inexhaustible fund of good nature made him a most agreeable companion to all. The Captain became much interested in the slate-writing phenomenon.

They arrived at Sydney on Thursday, September 19th, where they were welcomed by a few friends and members of the N. S. W. Association of Spiritualists. They remained in Sydney but one day, leaving on Friday evening for Brisbane, where they arrived late on Sunday night, much to the disappointment of a large number of friends who intended to meet them at the wharf, had they arrived in the afternoon, as expected. They were received by a delegation from the Brisbane Psychological Society, and other expectant friends, and conveyed to comfortable quarters. After a few days' rest they were accorded a public reception at Centennial Hall. The assemblage, we are informed by *Psychic Notes*, was thoroughly representative, including gentlemen holding high official positions, who are known to be greatly interested in psychological research. Mr. P. R. Gordon, the President of the Psychological Society, occupied the chair, and in a few opening remarks stated that "it was not intended that the present should be a large public gathering, but, rather, one of friends, who would accord a hearty fraternal welcome to our visitors from across the sea, and hence it has not been made public, and only privately announced." A short musical programme followed, in which several local artists took part. Then followed an address of welcome to Mr. and Mrs. Evans by Justice of the Peace, Mr. William Widdop. He assured them that they were heartily welcome to Queensland, and that all present that night would do their utmost to render their social surroundings as agreeable and pleasant as possible, etc. Mr. Evans briefly responded, saying he fully appreciated the kindness shown to himself and wife, and had no fear as to the success of his visit. Another short address by Mr. H. Burton then followed introductions and pleasant social intercourse, with a short programme of dances.

At a private, impromptu seance, held on Saturday evening following his arrival, with George Smith, Honorable Secretary of the Brisbane Psychological Society, and also editor of *Psychic Notes*, Mr. Smith says:

> We obtained a message containing 132 words, completely filling one side of a slate held in our own hands, in less than twenty seconds. Every word was neatly and distinctly written in lines as straight as a ruler. The ease and rapidity with which this writing appeared seems to preclude the idea that it is written in the ordinary way, and yet, when examined microscopically, the

traces of the pencil look exactly the same, as though written in the usual way by a human hand. We know these marvelous facts occur, but to learn by what law they are produced is the question which now troubles the psychological student. This was the first direct writing given to any sitter since Mr. Evans' arrival, and we duly appreciate the honor. It was a private message addressed personally to us, but also asked us to convey to all those friends who had assisted in bringing Mr. and Mrs. Evans to Brisbane, the hearty thanks of the medium's guides for affording them the opportunity of placing these great facts before the public of Australia, and assured us that we should soon obtain such results that would amply reward us for our labors in this cause. Mr. Evans then devoted the whole of the day, Saturday, September 29th, to representatives of the Brisbane press, who came in twos and threes throughout the whole day, and although Mr. Evans has hardly got settled after his long journey, the manifestations that occurred were highly satisfactory. Altogether, no less than twenty-four slates were carried away from his seance-room during the day, by representatives of the press.

As a rule, the Brisbane reporters were very exacting and critical. They had never seen any independent writing, and naturally believed it all jugglery. The *Brisbane Courier* published a long and very one-sided report of the experiences of its reporters, closing its review as follows:

> Then came a slight clicking like a telegraph instrument, but not nearly so loud, and Mr. Evans remarking, " Is that so?" informed me that I should not be able to get any further manifestations that day, and I accordingly left, taking the slates with me. There was certainly nothing in what was shown me to lead to the conviction that disembodied spirits had anything to do with the matter. The last quoted message is, I am certain, very different to what would have been conveyed to me, under the circumstances, by the gentleman who was supposed to have written it. At the same time I thought I could detect in it what might have been an influence of thoughts passing in my own mind whilst the writing was in progress. I have no other semblance of a theory as to the reasons of what I saw.

We may here remark that this reporter had had what to most people would have been proof positive of psychic power, such as writing in colors *over* a cross placed upon the slate, writing upon slates held in the reporter's own hand, etc. But to him it was all jugglery.

The Queensland *Figaro* tells the tale of its reporter's experience as follows:

* * * I expected to have been introduced to a gorgeously furnished house, full of possibilities for secret contrivances, and which I was prepared to regard as "readied up" for the occasion. Nothing could be farther from the reality. * * * The room in which the seance was held was almost destitute of furniture. * * * It remains for me to confess candidly that I went to Mr. Evans with a hostile intent, meaning, if possible, to prove him a fraud, and to expose any trickery or humbug, if such were present. * * * I had brought with me a book-slate that had been in use in my office for some years. It had been cleaned by myself, and was shoved up under my waistcoat. I had previously preferred the test to Mr. Evans that I might bring my own slate, and he had agreed to submit to the test. * * * This is what happened: Mr. Evans dropped a couple of grains of slate pencil into my slate, which I then shut up. I sat holding this slate in my hands quite three feet from Mr. Evans. * * * Presently Mr. Evans handed me a slip of paper and said, " Write down the names of one or two of your friends in the spirit-life, and lay the paper on the slate "—my book-slate, be it remembered. * * * I tried hard not to let Mr. Evans see the names I wrote down, and I believed I had succeeded. * * * My book-slate in the meantime had been lying on the table, but, as it was closed, it was safe. * * * Presently Mr. Evans said, "They're trying very hard to do something, but there is some difficulty. Open the slate." I opened it; on the second leaf of the slate was a thickly and heavily traced flourish, which might be taken for "Gray." Here I would like to say that the slate had never left my hands. When dropping in the grains of pencil, Mr. Evans *may* have touched the slate. If he did so the movement was so rapid that it escaped me. My impression at the time was that he did not touch it, but as I desire to account for that flourish by natural means, if possible, I give the reader every chance.

After describing different messages received on different slates in the usual manner, *Figaro* sums up as the others in favor of the conjuring theory; but his attempts at explanation only tend to increase the mystery surrounding the whole report, and leaves the reader with the idea that *Figaro* saw more than he could satisfactorily explain, his last few words containing some sound advice which his readers would do well to remember when reading his report: " Those who search after knowledge must inquire for themselves, and rest themselves entirely on their own experiences, perceptions, and judgments."

The *Southern World*, represented by Theodore Wright, reported as follows :

Mr. Evans, irritated with the *Courier* report (which had just then appeared) lifted his pile of slates upon the table for my inspection. They were simply a portion of a lot of slates he had bought wholesale in Brisbane, to meet the curiosity of inquirers, whom he suspected would seek him out. Nothing about them was in the slightest degree suggestive of trickery or legerdemain. Having examined the slates so as to be quite satisfied they had not been in any way manipulated beforehand * * * Investigation alone can solve the vexed and intricate problem. Those who are contented to pose as if only able to see this phenomenon from the standpoint of materialism and the gross trickery of legerdemain, simply write themselves down by so doing as fools and blind, or, to use the very expressive words of the medium—Mr. Evans—as "durned idiots," for everything is done by the medium so plain and unmistakably above board, without any pretense or effort whatever to disguise or conceal, that it is actually impossible to account for the phenomenon, save by some of the obscure and mostly ignored laws of the occult world, that is by psychology. Such as consent to view it pretensively otherwise, let themselves down immensely by so doing, and not at all those they are making a show of criticising.

The editor of *Psychic Notes* gives his own experience as follows :

On the morning the *Courier* report appeared, Mr. Evans was present in our office with a gentleman who had just had a seance, and who was showing the slates to several other persons in the room; some remark being made with reference to the production of writing on the slates without the aid of pencil, Mr. Evans volunteered an experiment there and then. One of the slates, perfectly clean on one side, was placed on the floor, with the clean side next the linoleum, and without pencil; one of the gentlemen present then placed his foot on the slate, and Mr. Evans placed his hand on the gentleman's shoulder; in a few seconds the slate was picked up, and on the under side was found written a name as though written with slate pencil. A short report of this fact, which occurred in the presence of six witnesses, was forwarded to the *Courier* but was refused insertion.

On Tuesday evening, October 4, 1888, we had a private seance with Mr. Evans, when something occurred worth recording, as follows : After cleaning wo slates in the usual way, we thoroughly satisfied ourselves that no mark was visible, placed one over the other and held them in our hands. After a few moments Mr. Evans remarked that writing had not yet commenced, and although he did not do this with all, he told us to open the slates and see for ourselves that nothing had yet been done to the slates. We did so, and the slates showed a perfectly blank surface; still holding them in our own hands we closed the slates together again, and in a few moments afterwards, being told to open them again, we found both slates filled with writing, one containing four messages in patch-work styles, the fourth being in printed letters, and in four different colors, from an American Indian chief, two miniature faces drawn in pencil, and some hieroglyphics. The other slates, and one lying face downwards on the table under the hands of our wives, containing a neatly written message of 296 words, addressed to us by the guide John Gray, contained some sound advice, some of which we reproduce. He says: "I am sorry to see that too many enquirers are adopting too rigid methods for beginners, and even so-called Spiritualists attempt and suggest conditions that they ought to know would sever the forces that we must draw from the mediums in order to produce these manifestations. Why do they not come in that frame of mind that would bring their spirit friends to them, and allow them (the spirits) to furnish their own conditions until they have manifested a few times, and have learned the *modus operandi?* Then suggest those rigid tests by degrees, instead of barring your doors and asking your friends to come in and see you. You know that many spirits here have never manifested before, and I can assure you that they find it very difficult even under the most satisfactory conditions; and you must know that I have worked hard to aid them, and will continue to do so if investigators will be a *little* reasonable in their search for spirit communion."

The *Telegraph* reports as follows:

Although it has been my lot, in the course of a somewhat checkered and varied career, to encounter men of many callings, it yet remained for me to meet a spirit medium. I have always regarded the ordinary seances as so much waste of time for a busy man, and the Slade exposures did not prepossess me in favor of slate-writing mediums in general. However, as several of my personal friends—including some of the best known and respected men in the city—had contributed to the expense of bringing over Mr. and Mrs. Fred Evans from San Francisco, I readily undertook the duty laid upon me to represent the *Telegraph* at Mr. Evans' Press seances on Saturday. I entered Mr. Evans' operating-room after the two visitors, who have described their experiences above. Seating myself opposite to Mr. Evans, he began by taking up a slate from an apparently inexhaustible store on the floor at his left hand. This he spat upon and rubbed with a cloth on both sides, explaining that he used spittle for magnetizing purposes. At his request I held the slate upright, pressing my fingers against each side. Mr. Evans did likewise for a few moments, and then repeated the process with another slate. I was, however, careful to keep an eye on the first slate during the magnetizing of the second. This over, Mr. Evans produced from a small box on the table an india-rubber band and a small pellet of pencil. The pencil was dropped on the first slate, the second slate was laid on top of the other, and the india-rubber band placed over both. This was done fairly over the middle of the table, and if any sleight-of-hand work took place it was much smarter than anything of the kind I have seen, and I have seen a good deal. The slates thus joined, I held them between the forefinger and thumb of each hand. Conversation on spirit matters was carried on freely, and Mr. Evans stated that he was very tired, and as he had been out of practice for two months, the exertions of the day had told upon him. During the conversation I tilted up the slates in my hand and distinctly heard the little pellet of pencil roll to the lower edge of the frame. Thenceforth I kept it there. When the slates were subsequently opened, a message was found written in crayon colors.

The Gympie *Times*, Queensland, says:

I have been present at one of Mr. Evans' seances, and I am bound to say it was different to the usual run of spiritualistic affairs. Everything was done in open daylight, and the slate-writing was not done under a table or by personal contact of the medium.

A gentleman of high, commercial standing in Brisbane called upon Mr. Evans for a private seance, on Friday, the fifth of October, and on a slate held in his own hands received a message in German, signed with the name of a deceased relative. The message contained forty-five words, neatly and accurately written, and, in the opinion of several German gentlemen who saw the slate, must have been written by a person thoroughly understanding the German language.

The Spiritualists themselves were extremely critical, often insisting upon the most crucial conditions, thereby erecting barriers of positive magnetism around the slates that made it very hard for John Gray to overcome them, and extremely wearing upon the psychic.

Mr. Evans relates that one of the chief difficulties he had to encounter at the crucial test seance he gave in Brisbane, Australia (mentioned hereafter), was the persistent disposition of the committee appointed to conduct the seance to open and examine the slates held in their hands.

It should be remembered that those slates had been thoroughly cleaned by the committee themselves, that they had placed bits of pencil between them with their own hands, and that the slates were not for a moment out of their hands.

Mr. Evans explained to them the conditions necessary to produce the writing, one of which was that the slates should be kept closed—that the opening of them exposed their inner surfaces to the light, which interfered with the collection of the spirit forces necessary to enable the spirits to communicate.

But it availed nothing. First one and then another, overcome by curiosity to know what was going on inside, would insist upon opening the slates. There was one sensible gentleman on the committee who obeyed instructions, and his slates were filled with writing, while the others got nothing. But this was sufficient for the object intended.

The history of this test seance is as follows: After Mr. Evans had left Brisbane for Melbourne, and, notwithstanding he had given a most satisfactory demonstration of independent slate-writing before the Society of Psychical Research of Brisbane, a fakir broke out in the local papers, claiming to expose Mr. Evans' method of obtaining the writing as a trick of jugglery. Upon his return to Sidney from Melbourne, Mr. Evans went back to Brisbane, hired a hall, and gave a free seance, all at his own expense. He challenged his accusers to come forward and make their charges true. It is enough to say that he put them all to rout by producing the writing upon slates in the hands of sharp-eyed skeptics, and under conditions where jugglery was simply impossible.

When preparing for this task his psychographic control,

Spirit John Gray, on being consulted in the matter, said, "Yes. I 'can get there,' but it will be hard on you." And, indeed, Mr. Evans states, it *was* hard on him. He was very sick during all of his return trip to Sidney, which occupied nearly two days, and he did not get over the effects of the seance for many days.

It is natural that good psychics should want to accept all challenges of their spirit powers, but we question whether it is wise for them to do so. Many Spiritualists, and all skeptics, have no idea of the delicate machinery of mediumship, or of the nature of the forces used to produce such wonderful results. Psychics themselves, and even their spirit guides, do not always understand these things. Hence it is that psychics of this class are often broken down and ruined by an over-straining of their powers.

And, after all, what good is accomplished? The very next fakir that comes along will demand a repetition of the challenge, and endeavor to use it as a means of free advertising to foist himself upon public attention. He can always find a church open to him, and some pious but ignorant minister ready to assist him with his show, which usually bears no more resemblance to genuine spirit manifestations than a dead donkey does to a live race horse.

We cannot afford to have our good psychics over-worked in trying to convince those who are not ready to be convinced. We need their powers for worthier ends. Hence we would urge all psychics to pay no attention to those who challenge their powers for the purpose of disproving them.

FRED EVANS BEFORE THE PSYCHOLOGICAL SOCIETY OF BRISBANE, QUEENSLAND.

[From *Psychic Notes*.]

WITH this issue of *Psychic Notes* we present our readers with an engraving of one of the two slates, obtained at the seance given by Fred Evans before the members of the Brisbane Psychological Society, on Wednesday evening, October 24, 1888, and which was briefly reported in our last issue, fuller particulars being held over until this issue. A special meeting of members only was called for this seance, strangers and visitors being excluded so as to have the most harmonious conditions possible. There were present about forty members, including the worthy president of the society, P. R. Gordon, Esq., who occupied the chair, and in a few words stated the object of the meeting, and called upon Mr. Henry Burton, a gentleman of great experience in psychological investigations, to deliver a short address preparatory to the seance. Mr. Burton, in a short speech, explained to his hearers the necessity for the observation of right conditions in an investigation of this kind, and how important it was that all antagonistic and inharmonious influences should be absent on such an occasion as the present in order to obtain the best results, and concluded by asking his hearers to patiently assist Mr. Evans in what was only an experimental seance, and not to be disappointed should a failure ensue.

Mr. Evans then came forward, appearing rather nervous at first, this being the first seance given in public by him for some months past. He had privately expressed his opinion, before entering the room, that he did not expect to get very good results, as he did not feel in the best of condition. Two of the gentlemen present, Mr. A. Ranniger and Mr. H. Phippard, having been selected a committee to superintend the preparation of the slates and act on behalf of the members, they, together with Mr. Evans, stood at a small table about three or four feet in front of the audience, each of the committee examining the slates as they were handed to them by Mr. Evans; and two pair of slates having been cleaned and prepared in this manner, and small pieces of slate pencil placed between each pair, they were carefully sealed together with sealing-wax. The two gentlemen, each holding a pair, then stood one on each side of Mr. Evans, in front of the table, and about two feet in front of the first row of chairs containing the audience. Mr. Evans

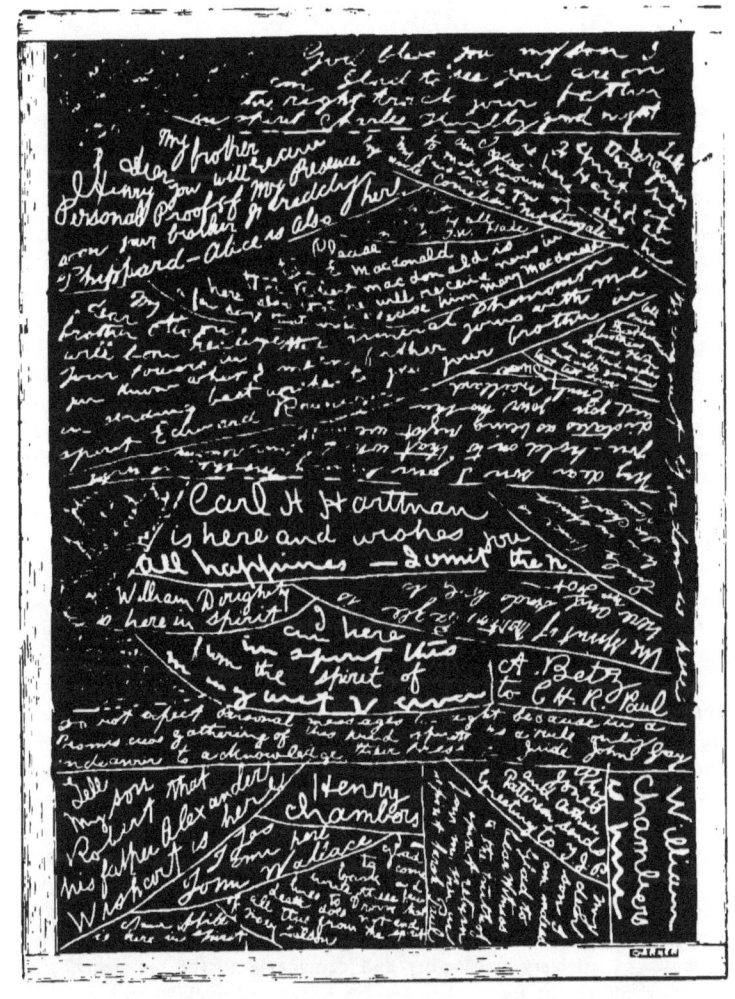

then connected himself with the slates by touching one edge of each pair of slates as they were held by the two gentlemen on each side of him. These two gentlemen then joined each his disengaged hand to the person's sitting at each end of the first row of chairs, and then all present in the room joining hands, a perfect chain was formed, thus making a connection of all present with the slates, and Mr. Evans standing between the two committee men, a strong power was at once manifested, some of the members being greatly affected, being twisted in their seats as by the power of a galvanic battery; several could not stand the power, and were forced to retire from the chain. One member became unconscious to what was passing, and knew nothing of what transpired until after the slates had been passed round for examination.

In a few minutes from the time the connection was made from the slates to the audience (certainly not more than five), Mr. Evans gave orders to break the seals and open the pair held by Mr. Ranniger, which was done, Mr. Ranniger finding one of the pair covered with colored writing, and a portrait in the centre; a murmur of surprise broke from the audience, who, however, still waited with joined hands the results on the other pair held by Mr. Phippard. About two minutes elapsed and then this pair was opened, the members having far greater cause for surprise at the results obtained in this pair, for one slate was found completely covered with writing, some in colors, but the most of it in slate pencil, some of the writing being so fine and small as to require the closest inspection to read it. No less than thirty different messages were found on this slate, a number of which were read out to the audience and recognized in nearly every instance. Some of the messages were addressed by name to members who were absent from the seance; others to gentlemen, who, though not members, were interested in other ways in the work of Mr. Evans. Some of the messages are so finely written as to contain from seventeen to twenty words in the space of about half an inch square. The engraving on the front page of this issue is a reproduction of this slate as near as can be done by the best available local talent; it is impossible to produce an exact *fac simile* of the slate, but our artist has succeeded in giving our readers a very fair idea of the original slate. Some of the messages are very satisfactory and convincing to the recipients. One gentleman informs us that before leaving home, and while at tea, one of his children remarked that Auntie Maggie would be sure to be there and write a message, and, sure enough, on the slate appears a message from the sister of the gentleman mentioned, and, of course, he was very pleased to be able to inform his child the next day that Auntie had written as expected. In the centre of the slate appears a message in colored writing:

    Carl H. Hartman is here and wishes you all happiness. I omit the " n."

At first we could not understand the last few words, "I omit the 'n,'" but after awhile we remembered that it had been remarked by some, who had seen a previous message from him on a slate, that he only spelled his name with one "n" instead of two, as it was supposed he should do; but in this message, as though to settle the matter and stop the discussion, he states that he omits the "n," thereby inferring that he knew of the remarks that had been made *re* the spelling of his name. On this slate also appears the following from spirit guide John Gray:

Do not expect personal messages to-night, because in a promiscuous gathering of this kind, spirits as a rule only endeavor to acknowledge their presence.

This remarkable slate contains about four hundred and fifty words, giving fifty different names, and is written in ordinary slate pencil and ten different colors. The other slate, which contained in the centre a remarkably well executed portrait of Pierpont (a somewhat similar picture of which appeared in a former issue of *Psychic Notes*, being an illustration of one of the slates obtained in the presence of Professor Alfred Russell Wallace at San Francisco), also contained six messages written round the edges of the slate between the portrait and the frame. These messages were written in brilliant colors, each message being recognized by some member present. Mr. Evans was as pleased as his audience at the result of this seance, and was the recipient of hearty applause and congratulations at the close of the meeting.

Psychic Notes also has the following to say of Mr. Evans:

COLOR TESTS AND PORTRAIT DRAWING.

At nine o'clock on Saturday morning, October 20, 1888, we (the editor of this journal) had an experimental seance with Fred Evans, and obtained on a slate held under our own hands a drawing, of which the accompanying illustration is a *fac simile* as near as can be produced in an engraving of this kind. We sat for whatever the guides of the medium were pleased to give us, and were more than satisfied with the results, which were simply marvelous. Mr. Evans first handed us a slate, which we satisfied ourselves was perfectly clean, and which after having been held edgeways between our fingers for a few seconds we placed flat on the table; another slate having been served in exactly the same manner, a small piece of pencil was placed between the two slates, and an elastic band having been placed around the slates they remained under our left hand until the seance closed. Another pair of slates, which we were also satisfied were perfectly clean, we fastened up as the first pair and placed them under our right hand; they also remaining there and not being moved until opened by ourselves. We then at the request of Mr. Evans took a small piece of paper, which we examined and found perfectly blank, and folding it up three or four folds tucked it in between the elastic band and the slate under our left hand, and placed our fingers on the paper. We are quite positive not a mark was on the paper when folded by us, and that the paper did not afterwards leave our possession until we unfolded it again. We then took a second piece, and examining it carefully folded this in like manner, Mr. Evans dropping a minute particle of lead pencil in between the last fold; this we also fixed under the elastic band and held it there with our fingers. After a few minutes' conversation, a rapping sound being heard on the slates under our right hand, Mr. Evans remarked that they were finished with that, and on removing the band we found on the under surface of the top slate the portrait of a relative of ours, of which the accompanying illustration is a copy. It is impossible to reproduce it exactly as it appears on the slate, it being a remarkable combination of slate and lead pencil—the surface of the slate being evidently whitened by slate pencil first and the portrait then artistically executed in lead pencil on the white ground, the name of the spirit artist St. Clair being neatly signed under the right-hand corner of the picture. Underneath appears the following message:

FRIEND SMITH:—We have given you this as a proof of our power to draw; this is only crude, because we cannot get the necessary force, but in a short time we will do better.

STANLEY ST. CLAIR.

Running along the edge of the slate on the left-hand side is a short message from Wm. Denton, the writing being remarkably small and fine. Along the right edge of the slate in printed letters appear the words,

Indian Jim come soon,

and some hieroglyphics we do not understand. At the top of the slate, in the left corner, is a combination of ten different colors, as brilliant as it would be possible to produce them with colored crayons; and to the right of the colors the following message written by guide John Gray:

FRIEND SMITH:—We have materialized these colors merely to show you what is possible under proper conditions. JOHN GRAY.

Before noticing all these particulars on this slate (which we did after the seance was over) we placed it on one side, still keeping our left hand on the other pair of slates and blank papers. Mr. Evans then suggested we should try a color test, and asked John Gray if he thought he could reproduce any of those colors from the slate on one of the pieces of paper which we held under our fingers. Having received in some occult manner an affirmative answer, he took the slate with the colors on and held it for a moment over the piece of paper, which lay between our fingers and the surface of the slate under our left hand. In ten seconds he said it was done, and on unfolding the piece of paper we found five of the colors reproduced on the paper, the words "Color Test" and "John Gray" being written, and several lines of color drawn across the paper. After placing this on one side, Mr. Evans asked us to open the other paper, and on this piece of paper, which only measures three inches square, we were surprised to find written small and neat in lead pencil three different messages and a miniature drawing of a man's head. One of the messages, in writing so fine that it almost requires a glass to read it with, is as follows:

MY DEAR FRIEND: We give you these few lines to prove to you that spirits can use paper as well as slates. JOHN GRAY.

Another message:

I am pleased to bear testimony to this important fact. WM. DENTON.

Another:

Carl H. Hartman is here.

A name, James Smith, and the miniature drawing, all produced in lead pencil, on a small piece of paper three inches square folded three times, and on which we can positively swear there was not a mark when we folded it up and placed it under our fingers. Shortly after this another rapping announced that the slates under our left hand were done with, and on removing the band we found the surface of one of the slates covered with a message containing one hundred and fifty-two words, being a private message to us from the medium's spirit guide, John Gray, in which he stated he hoped soon to give us some remarkable manifestations if the medium was kept in proper condition, and also that as the artist Stanley St. Clair had not exercised his power over the medium for about two months he had not done so well as he could and would do in the future. The seance at which these marvelous results were obtained then closed, having lasted altogether a little over half an hour. The slate containing the portrait and colors, and the paper with the writing on, may be inspected by anyone interested, at our office, and further particulars obtained if desired.

PAINFUL ACCIDENT.

MR. FRED EVANS met with a painful accident a few weeks after his arrival in Brisbane, which confined him to his room for several weeks, and part of the time to his bed. At the time of the accident Mr. Evans was, accompanied by two friends, returning to Brisbane from a trip to the Enoggera range of mountains, having left Brisbane the day before (Saturday). Mr. Evans having been very unwell a few days previously and feeling somewhat weak, was accommodated with a horse, and was riding slowly on, his two friends following on foot behind. The road was rough and very precipitous, and owing to a thunder-storm the night before, the ground in places was very soft and treacherous. Suddenly Mr. Evans heard the voice of spirit guide John Gray telling him to get off the horse, and in order to be ready to jump off at once Evans loosed his feet from the stirrups; had he got off at once the accident would not have happened, and, as it was, through being somewhat prepared by the warning, it was not so serious as it otherwise would have been. A few moments after hearing the voice, the earth gave way under the horse's feet on one side of the track, and Fred at once jumped off at the other side, and thus saved himself from falling with the horse and probably being crushed under it; but unfortunately in coming down he alighted with all his weight on a stone on the lowest part of the spine, and on his friends reaching him a minute later they found him stretched unconscious on the ground—the horse having meanwhile made off into the bush. The situation then was certainly very critical and alarming—no house nearer than Gold Creek Reservoir, two or three miles away; no conveyance; the nearest water half a mile away, and one of the party of three unconscious and seriously hurt. It would be difficult to analyze the feelings of Mr. Evans' friends at this moment, but we may be sure they both received a painful shock, and did all they could to relieve the sufferer. One of them carried water in his hat a distance of half a mile, while the other, who is possessed of considerable magnetic power, tried his best to bring back the vital spark of life that seemed to have left the inanimate form before him. After some time they were rewarded by Mr. Evans returning to consciousness, but only to find him in great pain and with his limbs partially paralyzed. And then commenced a terrible and painful journey to Gold Creek, which though short seemed ten times as far as it really was. Carrying and supporting the sufferer between them as carefully and tenderly as possible over the rough track, they at last reached the cottage at Gold Creek, where Mr. Thompson (the owner) did all in his power to assist them; and after using all the available remedies, thereby lessening the pain somewhat and partly bringing back the use of his limbs, Mr. Evans was carefully placed in a conveyance and brought on to Brisbane, arriving late at night. Dr. Taylor, who visited him next morning, found him (besides the injury before mentioned) suffering from a severe shock to the nervous system, and which seemed to have thrown his whole body out of order. He suffered severe pain, and was at one time in a very serious condition, but with the careful attention of Mrs. Evans and friends, and doubtless of his host of spirit friends, he rallied through the crisis, and when well enough was moved from Warry Street, where he resided, to a friend's house at Ashgrove, where, with plenty of fresh country air, sympathetic nurses, and every comfort, he soon recovered his usual robust health and strength, and was once more fit to fight the good fight of truth. This unexpected trouble was doubly unfortunate, because it happened just after that remarkable seance which Mr. Evans gave to the members of the Psychological Society, and when inquiries were beginning to be made by persons who at first doubted the reality of the phenomenon but were now beginning to look upon it more favorably.

EXPERIMENTS IN OTHER PHASES.

WE copy from *Psychic Notes*, of Brisbane, the following series of experiments with Mr. Evans, made by the editor of that journal. We may add that we have had similar satisfactory experiments with Mr. Evans, but prefer to let *Psychic Notes* tell the story.

EXPERIMENTAL SEANCES WITH FRED EVANS—MARVELOUS RESULTS.

[By the Editor of *Psychic Notes*.]

At 9:30 o'clock on Saturday morning, December 8, 1888, I called upon Mr. Evans at his rooms for the purpose of an experimental seance, my object being to try and obtain phenomena that would interest the readers of *Psychic Notes*. At first I felt doubtful of meeting with much success, this being my first seance since Mr. Evans' recent illness, but as events turned out I was rewarded with remarkable results. It is wholly unnecessary to describe the room in which this seance was held, except to state that it is an office rented by Mr. Evans in a large building full of similar offices; a few chairs and a deal-top table are all the furniture the room contains, and there was no other person present in the room during the seance.

EXPERIMENT NO. I.

We seated ourselves at the table, Mr. Evans with his back to a window overlooking the street and opposite to me. Two new 5x7 slates having been cleaned and examined in the usual manner, they were placed on the table. Mr. Evans proposed that we should try to get something on paper, and addressing spirit guide John Gray, Mr. Evans asked if we would be successful with a paper test, when three raps on the table gave an answer in the affirmative. Mr. Evans then asked me to tear five or six sheets of paper from a plain paper pad that lay on the table. I tore off five pieces, each measuring six inches long by three inches wide, and spreading them out and examining them closely could discern no mark of any kind whatever upon them. I then laid the five pieces of paper on top of one of the slates which lay on the table, and covering it with the other placed my hands on top, and did not again remove them from the slates for one instant until they were opened and the papers taken out. Mr. Evans placed a lead pencil on top of the slates and touched the slates at the edge next him with his fingers. I immediately felt a very powerful force of some kind passing apparently from my fingers to the slates, and experienced one very violent shock through my whole body, which jerked every portion of my frame from head to foot. Mr. Evans said the power was very strong, but as he had not tried the present experiment since he sat with Professor Alfred Russell Wallace, at San Francisco, and who obtained a similar test, he did not know whether it would be entirely successful or not. Again a rapping on the table announced that the results would be satisfactory, and shortly afterwards a distinct rapping right on the slates, apparently close to my fingers, informed us the work was done, the time occupied being under five minutes from when I placed the paper between the slates. I then removed the top slate, which had nothing upon it. The five pieces of paper lay just as I had placed them, one above the other, on the other slate. On removing and examining these pieces of paper, I found on four of them drawings of no less than seven different portraits or faces, the fifth piece being still blank as placed with the others.

EXPERIMENT NO. 2.

Having placed the papers containing the pictures on one side, leaving the close examination of them until after the seance, I turned up the remaining slate that lay on the table, and on the face next the table found a private message from John Gray, in which he says he intends giving several interesting tests to place before the world, through the medium of *Psychic Notes*. Then followed another very interesting experiment: Mr. Fred Evans gave me one of his cards, and holding a book in his hand, told me to push it at random anywhere between the closed leaves of the book. This I did, it being impossible for either to know at which page I had inserted it. The slate remaining, which had been used in the previous experiment, was placed on the table with a small scrap of pencil between it and the table. Mr. Evans then inquired from John Gray if he could produce, in writing on the slate, four or five lines from the page of the book where the card was inserted. A reply in the affirmative was at once given by audible raps on the table, and in less than three minutes another rapping signified that the test had been accomplished. On raising the slate I read these words : " The glorious sentence, 'God is love.' Here we have the sphere of truth; not a single hemisphere. We must wise as well as loving, intelligent as well as sympathetic, rational as well as emotional, before we can scale the pyramid and reach the apex of successful humanitarian endeavor." Underneath this was written, " The above is the top five lines, page 47, right page of the book. This will prove that we are an independent force, and do not depend on human knowledge for independent intelligence.—GUIDE JOHN GRAY." I then opened the book and found the card had been inserted at page 47, and that the top five lines on that page read as copied on the slate, with the exception that four words had been omitted on the slate. In the book, the words "God is wisdom" appear between the words "sentence," and "God is love;" also the word "be," between "must" and "wise."— "We must be wise." With this exception, the remainder is a correct copy of the five lines as they are printed in the book, which is entitled "The Spiritual Science of Health and Healing," by J. W. Colville. This satisfactory and successful experiment, proving the existence of an invisible intelligence, and of the possibility of obtaining writing that could not possibly be a reflex or an abstraction from the minds of the sitters, brought this interesting seance to a close.

DESCRIPTION OF THE DRAWINGS.

As mentioned above, four out of the five pieces of paper placed between the slates contained drawings. On one piece is a likeness, with the words "Your Uncle" written just underneath the face. This is a similar picture received by me through Mr. Evans some time ago. on a slate, and which was reproduced in No. 3 *Psychic Notes*, but on this paper, instead of the bust as shown on the slate, appears a female face, and the name "Emily" written underneath. In connection with this I may mention that at other previous seances, and through several different mediums, I have had described as standing near me a female spirit who gave the name of "Emily," a cousin; on this piece also appears the name "James Black." Another piece contains the outlines of a boyish face, underneath which is written "Cousin Henry." Not recognizing or knowing this "Cousin Henry," I showed it afterwards to my elder brother, who immediately remembered a cousin Henry who was drowned when a boy; my brother also informed me that the boy's father was the uncle whose picture I have twice received as mentioned above. The face on the paper is certainly that of a boy; underneath is written that it is a cousin named Henry; I afterwards find that I had such a cousin who met his death whilst a boy. This is a test of some importance, seeing that I could not possibly have been thinking of or expecting a communication from this relative. Underneath this picture is written, "I hope to be able to give you some experiences in the near future that will please you.—JOHN GRAY." On the third piece appears a well-executed portrait of the late D. D. Home, the well-known medium, a very similar picture to which was produced in the *Golden Gate*, San Francisco, which picture was originally produced on a slate. Underneath the picture is the signature, "D. D. Home," followed by the words, "Friend Smith, we have given you this picture of our late earthly co-worker, D. D. Home.—JOHN GRAY." On the collar in the picture is the name of the spirit artist, St. Clair; this name is signed in a similar manner on several of the other likenesses. On the fourth scrap of paper, three different faces are produced—Professor Hare, Benjamin Rush, and a female face not recognized. The pictures of both Hare and Rush have been produced before on slates, at seances in America, these being also the work of St. Clair, the spirit artist.

That seven drawings of this kind and the written messages were produced on four pieces of paper, which less than five minutes before were placed by me perfectly blank between two slates, is certainly phenomenal in the highest degree, but that such a fact occurred I know, and though all the world doubted, it would not affect that knowledge. By what unknown law they were produced, I do not know; the *modus operandi* has yet to be discovered, but that it was the work of an intelligence outside of either the medium or sitter, the evidence is very conclusive. Until some more reasonable and rational proof is given that it is otherwise, we therefore accept it as the work of the spirit artist, St. Clair, whose name is signed to the pictures, and accord him our best thanks for his work. The drawings are remarkable productions, although somewhat rough and crude in appearance, for though apparently done in lead pencil, they do not appear to have been drawn in the ordinary way by hand, the lines and penciling being very faint. They have a peculiar appearance, as though impressed, photographed, copied, or precipitated in some mysterious manner upon the paper. It must be remembered also that the papers were all one on top of the other, and that the time occupied in the production was less than one minute for each picture. The writing which appears on some of the papers has more the appearance of being written in the ordinary manner, being much more distinct than the pictures. Many of our readers will remember that Professor Alfred Russell Wallace, the eminent naturalist, received a similar test through Fred Evans, in San Francisco, there being also present at the seance Mr. John Wallace, Dr. Wooster, and the editor of the *Golden Gate*, all of whom testified and signed a declaration to the absolute genuineness of the phenomena, which phenomena now having been duplicated in our presence, we with pleasure also add our testimony to the fact.

PASSING MATTER THROUGH MATTER.

In order to give John Gray an opportunity to fulfill his promise to give something interesting for the readers of *Psychic Notes*, I called upon Mr. Evans again on Wednesday morning, December 12th, for an experimental seance, when the following phenomena occurred: Mr. Evans produced a

FOUR KNOTS TIED ON AN ENDLESS STRING BETWEEN TWO SLATES.
[The above illustration shows the string as it appeared when the slates were opened, also the card to which it was sealed and the piece cut from it.]

new piece of strong cord of close fibre, from which was cut a piece thirty-six and one-quarter inches in length. I held this in my hands for a few moments whilst Mr. Evans cut a piece of card in such a manner that one piece, which I kept, would fit exactly to the other after the experiment was over. I then held the two ends of the string (upon which there were then no knots) over the piece of card, while Mr. Evans sealed it firmly to the card. The string then hung in a loop from the card—no knots being visible—and the two ends fast to the card. The string and card were then laid between two slates and fastened with an india-rubber band, and after being held in my hands a few minutes was placed upon the floor two or three feet from the table. The usual signal having been given by raps that the experiment was finished, the slates were picked up, unfastened, and the string and card immediately examined. The cord was found sealed to the card exactly as when placed between the slates, but on the cord were four knots that certainly could not have been tied on that string by mortal hand after it was sealed to the card in the manner described. The illustration gives an idea of the appearance of the string after the experiment, and the manner in which it was attached to the card; it also shows the manner in which the card was cut in two, the two pieces fitting exactly when placed together after the seance. The original piece of card with string attached may be seen at this office.

PHYSICAL MANIFESTATIONS THROUGH FRED EVANS.

[By the Editor of *Psychic Notes*.]

ON Friday evening, December 21, 1888, a number of gentlemen met, at the invitation of Mr. Evans, at the residence of Mr. Phippard (contractor for the government buildings) for the purpose of attending a physical seance. The editor of this journal being one of the number, we are able to give our readers some particulars of the remarkable manifestations which occurred at this seance. The circle, including Mrs. Evans, who sat at one open end, consisted of five ladies and eleven gentlemen, sixteen in all. The room in which the circle sat was a drawing-room, divided from a dining-room by folding-doors. One of the folds being opened, a curtain was suspended at the opening, and the dining-room used as the cabinet. The members of the circle were seated round the room in horseshoe shape in front of the curtain, and with all hands joined it was impossible for any one to pass within that circle to the space between the circle and the curtain without breaking the circle. Anyone entering that space in front must enter by the curtained opening from the dining-room. About three feet in front of the curtain was placed a table, and on it placed an accordion, concertina, bell, tambourine, and a guitar. All being ready, a committee of five gentlemen, including the writer—the others all being influential and well-known citizens, holding high positions in society in Brisbane—were asked by Mr. Evans to enter the dining-room and thoroughly examine it to see there was no one else there but himself, and nothing which could be used in any way in the seance to follow. Having satisfied themselves in that respect, and sealed the only door which led into the dining-room with postage stamps, in such a way that if the door was opened it would be known afterwards, Mr. Evans then requested the committee to so secure him that he would be unable to move from the position they placed him in. To do this Mr. Evans produced a strong brass collar, which was devised by a member of the Academy of Sciences for the purpose of testing Mr. Evans' powers as a physical medium, and certainly, to all appearance, nothing better could possibly be made for the purpose it is intended. This collar was screwed to the wall of the room by a screw-staple, through the eyelet of which the collar passed. The collar could be forced open in front sufficiently to put it round the neck, the opening in front then being locked together by a patent padlock. There is then only one way of

[Brass collar with which Fred Evans was fixed to the wall during a physical seance on Friday evening, December 21, 1888. The keyhole of the lock sealed with an initialled postage stamp.]

getting out of that collar, and that is by unlocking the lock in front; to attempt to pull the staple out of the wall would mean strangulation. The writer was first secured to the wall by this collar, and found it impossible to release himself from the collar. Mr. Evans was then locked up in it, the key being kept by one of the committee. Another gentleman then sealed up the keyhole in the lock with a postage stamp, and initialled it privately to make certain the postage stamp was not removed. Mr. Evans now being secured, the gentlemen of the committee joined in the circle in front of the curtain, and the lights put out, the circle all joining hands. Almost immediately, the instruments were moved on the table, loud knocks heard, the bell loudly rung, and the accordion most beautifully played, seemingly all round the circle, and close to the faces of the sitters, the wind from the bellows being felt quite distinctly. The guitar was then played, and floated about the rooms, each sitter also being lightly touched by it on the knee. Next followed the concertina, and a voice, said to be that of John Gray, complained about its quality, it being rather out of tune. This direct voice was heard during the remainder of the seance—sometimes behind the curtain, sometimes just in front, and then again so close to one or other of the sitters as to quite startle those near. A musical box was placed on a table just inside the curtain in the diningroom, and it having run down, John Gray, in the direct voice, stated his intention of winding it up, and immediately the noise of the winding lever being rapidly moved was heard, the power with which it was done causing the box to knock on the table as it was moved, and the music was started again. Several of the instruments were manipulated at the same time, and once the noise was sufficient to give one the idea of quite an orchestra being at work. The accordion was certainly most artistically played, the power required for its manipulation seeming to be very great. Almost simultaneously with the playing of these instruments there suddenly appeared at the curtain a beautifully illuminated materialized form, which we were afterwards informed was that of the ancient Spartan king, Agesilaus. The figure was beautifully outlined in some luminous manner, a diadem on the head, and numerous decorations on the breast being very pretty. Advancing a few steps forward the figure shook hands with Mrs. Evans, and placed his hand on the head of one of the gentlemen present; bowing gracefully to the circle, the figure then retired behind the curtains. Following this several other indistinct forms appeared, but none so distinct as the first. After more manipulation of the musical instruments, and some conversation with John Gray, who played the accompaniment to a song on the concertina, orders were suddenly given to light up, and the seance terminated. The gentlemen who fastened up Mr. Evans then immediately went into the dining-room, and there found Mr.

Evans just as he had been secured. He was very white, and in a cold, clammy perspiration, and evidently very much exhausted. The seal over the keyhole of the lock was found just as it had been placed there before the seance, and the private marks intact. The seals were also found intact on the door of the room. Considering the state of Mr. Evans' health, the unsuitability of the climate at this time of the year for physical manifestations, and the fact that it is about two years since Mr. Evans gave his last physical seance, the results obtained at this seance were very satisfactory, and very startling and mysterious to those present who had not seen similar manifestations before.

SPIRIT PORTRAIT
Taken for the editor of *Psychic Notes*.
[see page 130.]

A SEANCE WITH FRED EVANS.

[From *Psychic Notes*.]

THE following interesting account of a seance with Fred Evans has been handed to us for publication, by a gentleman holding a responsible position in the civil service of the colony (it was first offered to the Brisbane *Courier*, but refused insertion):

"Most of my readers, no doubt, perused the several accounts of seances reported in the Brisbane *Courier* and *Telegraph* newspapers. Even the most adverse of these reports thoroughly proved to the intelligent reader that something occurred which could not possibly be accounted for by legerdemain. The opinions given by some of the writers may well be ignored entirely, as they fail to prove any trickery on the part of the medium, Mr. Evans. I decided to visit Mr. Evans and see for myself the psychographic phenomena said to take place in his presence. Accordingly, accompanied by a friend, we called upon him at his residence, but Mr. Evans being unwell that day, he refused to sit for us; several others who had arranged for seances that day were also disappointed. This has happened several times since Mr. Evans has been here. Now, why should it be requisite that the medium should be in good health in order to hold successful seances, if the phenomena are produced by sleight-of-hand? He did not appear to be very ill on the day he refused to give us a seance; still he took no fees from anyone that day, and therefore lost several guineas which he might have got had he been in proper condition to give seances.

"Now for the particulars of my seance. Before proceeding the second time to Mr. Evans' residence, I bought two slates in town, and placing two bits of red pencil and one bit of ordinary slate pencil, about an eighth of an inch long, between the slates, tied them together with a piece of string. Before tying them up I put my name, and also got one of my fellow officers to affix his initials on the wooden frame of both slates, and also made certain marks on the slates with a knife in order that we might identify them afterwards. I then wrapped the slates up in brown paper and again tied them with another string. In this form I took them to Mr. Evans, and was again accompanied by my friend. We were received by Mrs. Evans, who engaged us in conversation a few minutes until Mr. Evans came into the room. In reply to inquiries regarding his health, he said he still felt very unwell, but would go on with the seances. I entered the seance-room alone with Mr. Evans, he stating that in his then state of health it might be better that we sit alone; I carried my packet of slates with me. The room has two windows; an oblong, uncovered pine table stood with one end to one large window covered with a white blind, the other window, which is smaller, being partly covered with a muslin curtain. The seance took place in full daylight. Mr. Evans sat at one side of the table with his back to the small window, I at the other side with the large window to my right. Mr. Evans took my right hand in his right hand for a minute, during which time his hand and arm twitched convulsively. When he let go he exclaimed, 'You have grand magnetism; it is extremely soothing to me.' I then asked him if he found any great difference in the magnetism of different individuals, when he informed me that there was so much difference that some people almost racked him to death, and this explains why some people get such better results than others. I may state here that I have studied and practiced mesmerism, or animal magnetism, for several years, and have been the means of relieving much pain and suffering through its agency.

"I was about to remove the brown paper wrapper from the two slates I had taken with me, so as to leave the two slates simply tied together, and give free access to any magnetism that may have to penetrate the slates, when Mr. Evans said it was not necessary, and that I was to keep the slates tied up as they were in paper. He said he did not profess to *always* obtain writing on slates brought by sitters fastened up beforehand, or, in fact, on any particular slates, but the former is obtained if the magnetism of the sitter happens to be favorable, as it was in my case. He requested me to hold my slates on edge on the table for a minute or two, which I accordingly did, he just touching the edge of the frames next to him. I then laid the slates down at my left hand, and at his request wrote several names of deceased friends on a slip of paper, without allowing him so see what I was writing by keeping my left hand over what I wrote. I wrote four names on the paper, and folded it while still behind my hand, and held it in my left hand during the remainder of the seance. Mr. Evans then stood up, and taking my packet of slates by one corner, threw it on the floor (which was covered with oilcloth) some distance from the table. The slates lay there during the remainder of the seance, in full view all the time. Mr. Evans did not get off his chair again till the end of the seance, and he could not reach the slates without doing so. I can certainly aver that it remained where thrown till the close of the sitting. No one entered the room, Mrs. Evans being engaged in conversation with my friend in the next room during the whole time I sat with Mr. Evans.

"Mr. Evans then took a slate, evidently new, from a number of such, and after wiping it on both sides with a rag, placed a small piece of slate pencil on the table, and placed the cleaned slate over it. I then placed both hands on the slate, and also on two others which had been treated as the first; Mr. Evans did not touch these slates again until the end of the seance. Occasionally Mr. Evans would appear to listen and then mention a name, asking me if I knew such a person. He said he heard the name spoken as if through a telephone, and that sometimes a number of voices was heard at the same time, thereby causing confusion (persons using the telephone will understand this). The first name he mentioned he could not get the proper pronunciation of, but it was sufficiently near to one I had written for recognition; he also gave the initial of the Christian name correctly. One of the slates on the table when turned over revealed this name, signed at the bottom of a letter purporting to come from him:

Well, you have come at last, and right glad I am to meet you here. You must first know that I and the rest of the folks have found much happiness here, and intend soon to give you a proof of our presence by rapping at the head of your bed; you will realize that which you have long waited for, soon. E. C.

" Mr. Evans, looking towards me, then said he saw the spirit of a lady over my head, named Martha E. This was a sister of mine whose name I had also written on the paper, and another one of the three slates on the table, on which I had kept my hand the whole of the time, was turned over, and a letter, covering the whole side of the slate, and signed with my sister's name, appeared:

God bless you. I am now able to give you some proof that spirits can and do come back. I wish I could make you understand my happiness here; I can assure you that I would not come back to live on earth if I could. My only regret is in leaving loved ones behind; but I feel happy in knowing that we are not parted forever, but will all meet again to part no more. Love to all. From the happy spirit of MARTHA E——.

" The medium then mentioned another name which I had also written, Mrs. W——, and told me that Ellen and also Elizabeth F—— were with her, and also Mary F——; the latter, he said, appeared to have died at an advanced age. I thought of my grandmother, who was over eighty when she died, but I could not remember her Christian name. I afterwards asked my father, and found her name was Elizabeth—one of the names given—and that Mary was the name of a sister of my father's, who would be over eighty years of age if still alive, but he does not know if she is dead or living. The last two names mentioned by Mr. Evans, Elizabeth F——, my grandmother, and Mary F——, my father's sister, I had not written down on the slip of paper. Mr. Evans then gave another of the names I had written on the paper, E—— P——, a sister of mine who, he said, wished to know 'What about the baby?' This sister died about twelve years ago, leaving a baby nine days old, which another sister adopted; this niece of mine is still living. Mr.

Evans then asked me if I remembered Henry. I could not remember any relation of that name for some time, but after thinking awhile I remembered a cousin, Henry M'C——, whom I had not seen for over thirty-six years; then he said, 'Do you remember William, a brother to Henry?' I then recollected a cousin Henry who came to Queensland and went up North; I do not know whether he is dead or alive, and cannot at present ascertain. Mr. Evans then told me I should hear some good news in a few days, and also that I would take a long journey from Brisbane shortly. The first I hope may be true; the latter I have no idea of at present. All this time my tied up slates had lain where they were put on the floor, and had certainly not been touched. Mr. Evans said he heard rapping on them, and getting up picked them up and placed them on the table by my side, still tied up in the brown paper I had brought them in. The medium then asked 'Johnny' if anything had been done with them, and immediately came a rapping on the table which he informed me was an answer to the effect that writing had been obtained on my slates, and requested me to open them, which I did; after taking the first string and paper wrapper off I found the string round the bare slates exactly as I had put it on. When I had removed that and opened the slates, I found writing on both slates in red and also slate pencil. On examination I found *facets worn on both particles of pencil*, proving that they had been both used. The messages read as follows (in red pencil):

  God bless you. I am glad to have given you these few lines to prove that Spiritualism is true. I have written with your pencil as an extra proof. This from your cousin. (Love from Mrs. W——).   Henry F——.

  (In red pencil): Your sister, R. P——, is here and wil control you to write soon. Love to all. From your sister,   R. P——.

  (In slate pencil): What more proof do you want?   John Gray.

"I leave my readers to decide for themselves how the writing was done, and admit that I cannot myself explain it, not having come to any decision as yet on that point. I am fully convinced that Mr. Evans did not write one word that appeared on my slates, but I give no opinion as to the source of the manifestations. I may state, however, that although the writing appears at first sight to be in different hands, it all has a resemblance in the character of many of the letters. This is not very strange, however, and is easily understood by the psychologist, seeing it comes through one medium or channel, and is likely to partake of his organism.   H. W. Fox.

  "Declared before me at Brisbane, this nineteenth day of October, 1888.
            "E. MacDonnell, J. P."

MR. EVANS' DEPARTURE FROM BRISBANE.

BEFORE taking their departure from Brisbane, the Psychological Society of that city extended to Mr. Evans a most cordial endorsement of his wonderful gifts, not only in words, which have the ring of the true coin, but in a purse of sovereigns also, as follows :

TESTIMONIAL.

(Psychological Society, Brisbane, Queensland, January 2, 1889.)

TO MR. AND MRS. EVANS, OF SAN FRANCISCO.

DEAR SIR AND MADAM :—We cannot permit your present visit amongst us to come to a close without expressing to you our earnest wishes for your future happiness and prosperity. We sincerely regret that, owing to your late unfortunate accident, and the depressing atmosphere of the hot summer months, conditions have not been entirely favorable to the highest manifestation of your psychic gifts, but many of us have witnessed more than enough to assure us that psychological students have in you superior instruments through whom they may obtain phenomena of the greatest importance to mankind. Without wishing to detract from the pleasure of others in Australia who are desirous to welcome you, we hope the time will not be long before you may be permitted to again visit us, when you may depend upon the reception always accorded to honest workers in the cause of truth by the liberal thinkers of Brisbane. But wherever you travel, or in whatever part of the world your lot may be cast, you will be followed by the heartfelt wishes for your highest happiness of the many friends who have derived pleasure and enlightenment from your visit. We also request your acceptance of the accompanying purse of sovereigns, contributed by a few friends on the eve of your departure for Melbourne, as some slight recompense for losses occasioned by the before-mentioned accident. With renewed assurances, believe us to be, dear sir and madame,   Very sincerely yours,

(Signed) WILLIAM WIDDOP, Chairman,
GEORGE SMITH, Hon. Sec.
On behalf of the meeting.

After Mr. Evans left Brisbane for Melbourne, a juggler named Patterson obtained access to one of the local papers, the

Telegraph, and gave a pretended *exposé* of Mr. Evans' method of procuring the writing. His articles were published with sensational head lines which were in no sense sustained by the matter which followed. The *Telegraph* also offered a challenge of one thousand pounds to Mr. Evans if he would produce the writing on the editor's own slates. Mr. Evans wrote back to the Psychological Society in Brisbane, instructing them to procure the *Telegraph* man's proposition in writing, when he would immediately go back to Brisbane and convince him of his error. But it was demonstrated that he was not willing to make good his boast. And the Psychological Society instructed its secretary to write to Mr. Evans, informing him of the failure of their committee to secure the signature of the *Telegraph's* editors to the one thousand guinea offer. The society expressed their continued confidence in Mr. Evans' psychographic powers, and in his honesty, and renewed their invitation for another visit from this psychic, which was accepted with grand results, as will be seen later.

Mr. Evans had already given a test seance to the Society for Psychical Research of Brisbane, as well as to many careful and skeptical investigators, and invariably with the most satisfactory results. Hence the pretended *exposé* created no little excitement in Brisbane. An officer was sent on to Melbourne with a view to his arrest, provided he should find the writing to be produced in the manner claimed by Patterson. Of course, it was not so produced (that is, by trickery), and he returned a convert to the truth.

After returning to Sydney, Mr. Evans went back to Brisbane (two days' ride by rail), for the purpose of confounding his accuser. He hired a hall, challenged honest investigation of the phenomena witnessed in his presence, and gave a free public seance. A committee of five persons were selected from the audience. The result was a grand victory for the spirit powers attending Mr. Evans. Just before leaving Brisbane Mr. Evans was waited upon by four members of the committee who conducted the public test seance. " They informed him," says the *Harbinger of Light*, "that as soon as he left it was the intention of Mr. Patterson to take exception to the conclusiveness of the tests then obtained, on the ground that Mr. Evans had furnished the slates, and requested him to give them a seance there and then, and obtain writing on two slates they had brought with them. Mr. Evans and the whole party retired into an empty room, and the four members of the committee holding the two slates in their own hands, obtained several messages on them, some of the messages being signed by relatives of the persons holding them. *The room did not contain one particle of furniture, and the slates brought by the committee never left their sight from the time of their arrival till the completion of the messages.* No more complete test than the above could possibly be given. The Pattersonian *exposé* vanishes before it into thin air."

Upon this subject the *Harbinger of Light* has the following:

A full report of Mr. Evans' address at West's Hall, Sydney, has reached us just as our paper is ready for press; but for this we should have been very pleased to have published it, as it contains a detailed account of the Patterson *exposé* business, of which we will give the gist, though we think what we have already written on the subject should have been sufficient to satisfy any unprejudiced person of the insufficiency of Mr. Patterson's theory to cover one-half the ground.

First—Patterson had only one sitting with Mr. Evans (October 3, 1888), when he expressed his opinion that "the manifestations were wonderful;" but pointed out that conjurers did many wonderful things, including slate-writing. Mr. Evans thereupon explained the three methods by which the latter was done, one of them being the "masked" slate, the latter appearing the most satisfactory to Patterson.

Second—Mr. Evans did not leave Brisbane till January 3, 1889, previous to which the genuineness of his mediumship was endorsed by the Psychological Society, who also presented him with a purse of sovereigns.

Third—No attempt at exposure was made until nearly three months after Mr. Patterson's sitting, and at least a fortnight after Mr. Evans had left Brisbane.

Fourth—It was known that Patterson had offered his professed discovery to the *Courier* for £50; but that journal having refused to have anything to do with it, the *Telegraph* had bought the sole right to publish it for a less amount. That it was purely a business transaction was shown by the fact of their copyrighting it, which they certainly would not have done had they published it on public grounds.

Fifth—That when the *Telegraph*, in a spirit of bravado, had offered a thousand guineas if Evans could produce a spirit writing on slates provided by them, Mr. Evans wrote to the Secretary of the Psychological Society, asking that body to wait upon the editor and request him to put the offer in writing, when Mr. Evans would immediately come from Melbourne to accept the challenge. That on compliance with this request the Secretary and other members called upon the editor, but could not induce him to write the challenge.

Sixth—That *no one who had sat with Mr. Evans* could be found to endorse Mr. Patterson's imitation, and that four out of the six persons who signed the account of the Patterson mock seance were shareholders in the *Telegraph!*

Seventh—That the said paper circulated a report that Mr. Evans had taken the first steamer to America, whilst he was giving successful seances in Melbourne.

Eighth—That the Psychological Society held a meeting to consider the matter, expressed their continued confidence in Mr. Evans; that a deputation was appointed to wait upon the editor to arrange for space to reply to his charges against Evans, but were refused such space.

Ninth—That copies of the *Telegraph* and *Week* (which belong to the same proprietary), containing the alleged *exposé*, were sent all over the world, and to editors of spiritualistic papers, to the detriment of Mr. Evans' reputation, and that *Light*, a London journal, was evidently misled by them.

The foregoing is the gist of the address, which pretty conclusively shows that the *exposé* was a job got up to make money at the expense of Mr. Evans' reputation.

WHAT MR. SOMERVILLE SAYS.

AMONGST the numerous testimonies to the convincing nature of Mr. Evans' mediumship that have come under our notice, aside from our personal experience, the following, extracted from a private letter to Mr. Carson from a former resident in Melbourne—Mr. A. Somerville—is a good specimen:

You say that you expect to go to China and Japan, and be absent till December next. I am sorry that this occurs at the time, as Mr. Fred Evans and wife expect to be in Australia; he is going (I understood) to Brisbane first and then to Sydney. I would be sorry that anything should prevent him visiting Melbourne, for I am sure that those who have any faith in progressive spiritual views would be pleased with his abilities. I visited him some months ago, and got the greatest satisfaction I could expect. He had never seen me before, nor had I seen him; I did not give my name either, first. I sat down at a small table; he went to the opposite side and was cleaning two slates, when he said, "There is a lady by your side who gives her name as Harriet," asking if I knew one of that name. I assented. "She says she is your wife, is that so?" I assented. "There is a young man with her who gives his name as George," did I know him? I assented. When the slates were ready, he put a very small bit of slate pencil between, and put a rubber band around both. I told him I had some questions on paper—five in all—some of them double, and all to my wife. He told me to put them all under the band. I did so, and put the points of my fingers on the slates as they lay on the table. He then got two other slates and laid them on the floor; then he sat down and we conversed on various subjects for fifteen or twenty minutes, when he said, "The answers are on the slates." I took the paper of questions out and put it in my pocket, and was about to read the slates from the table, when he said, "Read this from the floor first," which I did. The under slate had a message of welcome and congratulation from my wife, written on the upper side only—nothing being on the upper slate. Then I read the under slate which was on the table; it was filled on both sides with complete answers to all my questions, and *numbered consecutively*. On the under side of the upper slate was a communication from my son, unsolicited, and I had no thought of asking of any but my wife. Then I asked if Evans would enquire what was the illness that caused my wife's death. After a little while he replied, "She says it was so dreadful that she does not wish to refer to it." (It was cancer of the stomach.) I then asked if I could get a communication from a Dr. Dewolf, by whose advice I first went to see a medium some twenty-four years ago. Fred Evans asked his guide to see if he could bring Dr. Dewolf, and after a little, Fred Evans laid a slate on the floor, and soon there was a message on it quite characteristic of the man:

  Hello, friend Somerville, you have our best wishes for your future welfare. You now see that Spiritualism is all O. K. We cannot write more at present.   DR. C. DEWOLF.

This ended my first and only visit to Mr. Evans, which was to me thoroughly satisfactory as far as it went. I brought with me the four slates, with the messages written on them, and have them now. I omitted to say that the writing by Dr. Dewolf was each line alternately in *red* and *green*.

FRED EVANS IN MELBOURNE.

THE *Harbinger of Light* and *Psychic Notes*, as well as the secular press of the principal cities of the Australian colonies, were so loaded with Fred Evans and his seances during his memorable stay in the colonies, that if we should undertake to give a liberal fraction of their reports, this book would far exceed its intended dimensions. We can only relate the more important events as given by the local press.

The following, from Mr. Terry, editor of the *Harbinger of Light*, illustrates some of Mr. Evans' first work in that city:

Mr. and Mrs. Fred Evans arrived in Melbourne, by Sydney express, on January 10, 1889, and were met at Spencer Street by the President, Treasurer, and Secretary of the Victorian Association of Spiritualists. In the evening of the same day they were introduced to the members and their families at the Thistle Company's Hall. Although the meeting was hastily convened, there were about eighty persons present, and the utmost harmony and good feeling prevailed.

Mr. Terry, the President, in opening the proceedings, stated that they would be quite of an informal character. They had met to welcome Mr. and Mrs. Evans, whom he now introduced to them collectively, and hoped to do so individually further on. Mr. Evans had a world-wide reputation; he would be known to the readers of the *Harbinger*, the American and also the English papers, as a medium of exceptional powers and unsullied reputation. Physical phenomena alone, though an essential basis in many instances whereon to build the philosophy of Spiritualism, were very much lessened in value by the facility with which they could be counterfeited; but Mr. Evans fortunately combined both physical and mental mediumship, giving tests through the latter of spirit identity; and his work here was, therefore, likely to be of substantial benefit in the advancement of Spiritualism.

Mr. Evans briefly responded, expressing his satisfaction at the cordial welcome accorded to himself and Mrs. Evans, and giving a *resumé* of his experiences in Brisbane, where press antagonism had at first impeded his way. He had, however, in spite of unfavorable circumstances, succeeded in convincing a number of intelligent people of the reality of the phenomena, and the press had published the report of the local Psychological Society, which was endorsive of the genuineness of the phenomena. * * *

Early on Monday following the above, we received information that both Mr. and Mrs. Fred Evans were seriously ill, and on proceeding to the Federal Coffee Palace found them suffering from fever and ulcerated throats. Magnetic treatment, however, told rapidly on the fever, and by Wednesday they were sufficiently convalescent to be removed to Caulfield, where pure air and attention completed their restoration, and on Saturday Mr. Evans felt sufficiently well to give his first seance in Victoria, which took place in the writer's dining-room at Caulfield, there being present, besides Mr. and Mrs. Evans, Mrs. F. Harris, Miss S., Mr. Terry, his son and daughter. A Star lamp, giving a powerful light, was on the table. Mr. Evans produced two new slates which he, however, cleaned on the table, requesting the writer to hold them between his hands for a short time. Having done so we handed them back to him, and after placing a small grain of pencil between them, he passed a strong elastic band around them, and requested us to hold them edgewise on the table, and the remainder of the sitters to form a chain by connecting each other's hands. He then stood behind the writer, resting one of his hands lightly on our right shoulder, about two feet from the slate. Presently a faint sound of writing was heard, which lasted about two minutes, and when it ceased Mr. Evans took the slates, still closed and fastened, in his right hand, and rested them successively for about a minute on the shoulders of the remaining sitters, then handing them to us to open. On removing the bands one slate was found to be entirely filled with writing, the upper portion being written small, but very clear and distinct. It read as follows:

FRIEND TERRY:—I am pleased to greet you with these few lines, and desire you to have many seances with the medium when he becomes settled. I think it advisable that he should not give any seances until he has been settled in permanent quarters, which will be early next week. You will readily understand our motive for this. Accept the thanks of the spirit world for your kindness to our mediums. You will be amply repaid soon. Your son R——, and daughter M —— will develop strong medial powers soon. Good-bye for the present.

JOHN GRAY.

The next message was in a totally different hand-writing, as follows:

DEAR JENNIE:—Cheer up, lass, the dark clouds are dispersing, and all looks bright ahead. Love to the children. Your husband, THOMAS HARRIS.

Mrs. Harris asserts that the writing was a *fac simile* of Mr. Harris', though she had no letter at hand to show the correspondence.

To the right of this is a short message for Miss S., signed with the name of her grandmother. Between these in a triangular space is the following, written very small: "The spirit of E—— L—— is here, and sends love to Mr. Terry." Mr. Terry was the only person present who knew the spirit when in the body, and had not thought of her or mentioned her name for probably a year or more. Another message, very boldly written, announced that John Terry and many others who could not write now, but would make themselves known through the medium at a future time, were present. Then two lines as follows : " My love to you, uncle, and to cousin M—— and B——. From your nephew, 'Tom.' " The words " no more to-night " filled the slate, and finished the communication. During the whole of the sitting the slates never left the sight of any at the table, and Mr. Evans' hand was only in contact with the outside of them whilst they rested on the shoulders of the sitters during the reception of their respective messages.

On January 22nd, a party of ladies and gentlemen, numbering over twenty, met at Caulfield to spend a social evening with Mr. and Mrs. Evans. In the course of the evening Mr. Evans kindly offered to try an experimental sitting in the presence of the whole company, provided a suitable apartment were available. An enclosed veranda, being devoid of furniture, was decided upon as the most suitable, and the company, to the number of twenty-six, were seated in four rows, two small tables being placed about six feet from the front row, on one of which was placed the lamp, and on the other five blank slates, pencils; a glass of lemonade (brought in mistake for water) was used by Mr. Evans, who stood on the further side of the table, to wash the slates with. After having asked some of the sitters to touch the slates to magnetize them, Mr. Evans took an uncut slate pencil and drew two lines from corner to corner, intersecting each other at the centre; then dropping two small grains of the pencil on the linoleum, midway between the table and the sitters, he put a slate over each with the line side downward. Two other slates were put together with pencil between, and an elastic band round, and placed in the hands of Mrs. Harris, who was directed to hold them up over her head, and in the full light of the lamp. Mr. and Mrs. Evans, who were about six feet from either slate, were both powerfully affected for some three minutes of silence which ensued. We were then requested to lift one of the slates from the floor, and on doing so found it full of writing, in different colors. We immediately handed it to a well-known literary gentleman to take charge of till read; and the second slate being found blank, we took the closed slates from Mrs. Harris' hands, and on removing the band found one of the slates filled with writing. We immediately closed these and handed them to a legal gentleman, and the seance having finished, the holder of the first slate was requested to come forward to the table and read it. Although only the piece of ordinary slate pencil had been underneath the slate, the writing was in four colors, and read as follows:

DEAR FRIENDS:—I am pleased to meet you all here this evening. Many of you no doubt remember me, and my recent visit, when in the form, to your colonies. I have just come here this evening to ask you to appreciate these mediums' visit among you. Try and make it pleasant for them, so that they may come here again, and induce others to come and spread the grand truth of spirit return. The spirit world always recognizes and appreciates any kindness shown to their mediums, for it makes them better by being thus pleased and harmonized to be used as instruments of the spirit world, and I must say in conclusion that if these mediums are properly treated they will do much good, and make many hearts happy among you in the knowledge that your loved ones can and do come back. Good-night. WILLIAM DENTON.

This communication is undoubtedly written *over* the crossed pencil lines which were marked on the slate immediately before it was placed on the floor, and hence must have been written whilst the slate lay on the floor, several feet away from Mr. Evans, and in full view of at least a dozen of the sitters. Noticing a similarity to Mr. Denton's style in the writing, we subsequently looked up some of his letters received during his journey northwards *en route* to New Guinea, and find a very close resemblance between the two. The other slate contained no less than fourteen messages, addressed to different persons present, which want of space prevents our copying; enough, however, has been given to make manifest the particularly clear and satisfactory nature of Mr. Evans' mediumship, of which we shall have more to say in our next.

A very clever gentleman at Brisbane, Patterson by name, has found out "how it is done," and shown the method to several other gentlemen who have *not* had sittings with Mr. Evans, and who though signing a description of Mr. Patterson's performance as correct, are very careful to say that *it is alleged* that the various incidents in the mock seance are the same as those that occur at Mr. Evans'. The process is very simple: you have only to get your messages written beforehand, cover them over with another thin, frameless slate, exercise a little sleight-of-hand to put this out of sight during the seance, and there you are!!!

The Brisbane *Evening Telegraph* has gone into partnership with Mr. Patterson in the business, copyrighted their paper, and we presume intend taking out a patent for the invention. It may be new to them, but it is a very stale thing amongst conjurers and slate-writing imitators in America. It is very easy to gull the uninitiated and inexperienced with an explanation of this sort, or to persuade one here and there who has had a single seance that his senses have deceived him, but to the practical investigator, or clear-headed experimenter, the explanation is ridiculously thin.

Intensely clever people of the Patterson stamp imagine that they who fail to see as they do are brainless fools, and pit their half-hour's experience against the careful examination of men like Robert Dale Owen, William Crookes,

Professor Hare, and Alfred Russell Wallace, F. R. S., with the most unblushing effrontery. It pleases them and "tickles the groundlings," but has little effect on thoughtful men.

The following, from the *Harbinger of Light*, of March 1, 1889, illustrates another phase of the mediumistic power of Fred Evans:

Mr. Evans commenced his private sittings at 255 Victoria Parade, on Thursday, January 31, 1889, and has since been fully occupied. The serious fall he sustained in Queensland has materially weakened his nervous system, and necessitated the limitation of the number of sittings he is so able to give, hence many have had to wait their turn for a seance. We have conversed with several sitters, who have all been satisfied with their seance, and some of them quite delighted with the proofs of identity they have received from spirit friends. We have had two private sittings with Mr. Evans, on both occasions receiving conclusive tests; in one instance from a friend whom we were not thinking of, who wrote a message of nearly 200 words on a pair of slates placed on the floor about four feet from the medium. This message referred to matters known only to the communicating spirit and ourselves—events that occurred some five years since, and which were only recalled to memory by the communication. A gentleman well known in banking and commercial circles in Brisbane, who had had his faith shaken in the genuineness of Mr. Evans' phenomena by the Brisbane *Telegraph* articles, which untruthfully assert that Mr. Patterson obtains the same results by trickery, visited Mr. Evans in Melbourne during the early part of the month, and having obtained writing on his own slates under strict test conditions, has returned to Brisbane and published his experiences in the *Telegraph*, of February 9th, to the chagrin of Pattersonians. * * *

In *Psychic Notes* for January is published a description of a seance with Mr. Evans for the evolution of psychic phenomena, accompanied with an illustration of a collar and padlock, used to secure the medium during the seance, and prevent any possibility of his aiding the manifestations by any physical means. The precautions taken were deemed satisfactory to the committee who superintended the seance, but exception was taken by outsiders, first, to the security of the keyhole of the lock, which had been covered with an initialled postage stamp, and which it was asserted might have been moistened, removed, and reattached during the darkness; and, secondly, of the lock itself, which it was alleged might be picked with a penknife. We think most of our readers will join us in discrediting the idea that a patent lock with a keyhole three-eighths by one-sixteenth of an inch could be so opened without ocular demonstration of the fact, but as the possibility of picking the lock depends upon the keyhole being accessible, it is not necessary to consider this question in a case where precautions were taken to render the keyhole absolutely inaccessible to a penknife or any other instrument without certain detection, as in the case we are about to describe of a seance held at 84 Russell Street, on Friday, February 15th.

The seance was intended to have been held in our office, but there being greater conveniences in the library of the Association, it was determined to hold it there. Mr. Evans was not aware in what room it was to be held, and had never been in the room until he entered it to give the sitting. In the northwest corner of this room the framework of the cabinet used by the committee for Mr. Spriggs' materialization seances still remains. The curtains were attached to this, and in the extreme corner a pole about two inches in diameter was fixed to the wall by three iron staples, and screwed to the floor and upper frame of the cabinet.

The company present, in addition to the medium, consisted of Mr. John Carson, Mr. W. Morgan, Mr. W. H. Terry, Mr. C. Bamford, Mrs. H. Bamford, and Mrs. Evans. The apparatus to be used to secure Mr. Evans consisted of a brass collar made of stout wire, on which was threaded a brass eyelet staple with a single screw, one inch long in the worm, and a patent brass spring lock used for a similar experiment by a committee of the Academy of Sciences. The collar having been screwed securely into the pole by Mr. Bamford, and tested as to its security by the other gentlemen present, Mr. Evans sat on a plain wooden chair placed beneath it, whilst the collar was placed round his neck and fastened with the lock. It was found to be uncomfortably tight, however, and two books were placed under the front legs of the chair, to make his position more tolerable. A small piece of paper was then placed over the keyhole, and wax melted over it to a diameter of three-quarter inches. A seal half-inch in diameter was then firmly impressed upon it, and examined separately by the four witnesses, who, having each satisfied himself of its soundness, withdrew and closed the curtains.

The table had previously been put at the further end of the room, eight feet from where the medium sat, and on it were placed a large musical box, an accordion, a tambourine, and a common house-bell. The sitters arranged themselves in a section of a circle on the side of the table furthest from Mr. Evans, with hands joined, Mrs. Evans being in the centre, her hands held by Messrs. Morgan and Terry, and, having extinguished the light, the musical box was set going, and by request a song was started, but before the first verse was finished the accordion and tambourine ascended and began playing, and the bell was rung. When these ceased, a voice addressed Mr. Carson, saying the speaker was glad to see him again. Mr. Carson recognized the voice (which was a peculiar one) as belonging to John or Johnnie Gray, whom he had seen materialized at Chicago in 1876.

John reminded Mr. Carson that he had spoken disparagingly of his voice on that occasion. This Mr. Carson remembered to be a fact.

Presently the accordion rose again from the table, and played with power and precision, " Home, Sweet Home." The tambourine and bell joined in, and the musical box was thrown violently on a chair, while a clatter as of booted feet was heard upon the table. The instruments having descended upon the table and floor, the voice of John Gray informed us that through the medium not having taken rest from his labors prior to the seance, the power was exhausted. A light was accordingly struck, and Mr. Evans found seated with the collar round his neck, as before the seance. The seal over the keyhole was carefully examined and certified to be intact. It was then cut off by Mr. Terry, but the wax having burnt through the paper into the keyhole, it had to be picked out with a knife before the key could be inserted. Mr. Evans, when released, was much exhausted. There was not the slightest possibility of Mr. Evans physically aiding the phenomena that occurred, and as the two end-men of the chain of sitters, Messrs. Carson and Terry, placed both their hands in contact with that of the next sitter's during the whole of the seance, there was no free hand in the room. The door of the room was locked and the key in the possession of Mr. Morgan, who is only an investigator of psychic and spiritual phenomena. The result of this seance should establish the genuineness of the similar one held in Brisbane, by demonstrating that the removal of the seal, or release of Mr. Evans, is not essential to the occurrence of phenomena.

PUBLIC DEMONSTRATION OF PSYCHOGRAPHY AT HORTICULTURAL HALL, MELBOURNE.

[From the *Harbinger of Light*.]

ON Sunday, March 10, 1889, Mr. Fred Evans gave his services to the Victorian Association of Spiritualists for a public demonstration of his wonderful mediumistic powers at their evening service, held in the Horticultural Hall, Victoria Street. The hall was crowded in every part, a large number standing in the doorway and central aisle.

The proceedings were opened, as usual, with a hymn, followed by an excellent trance address by Mrs. T. Harris.

At a quarter to eight o'clock Mr. Evans ascended the platform, and, being introduced to the audience by the Chairman, Mr. Terry, said there were three things essential to success in these experiments—that the medium should be in good health, free from mental perturbation, and that the audience should be passive and orderly. The first two of these conditions were absent; he was not in good health, and had sat up all night tending his wife, who was seriously ill, which had naturally disturbed his mental condition. He would, however, do his best, though he could guarantee nothing.

He requested a gentleman and lady to come forward to the platform on behalf of the audience. Two gentlemen, Mr. J. Henshaw and Mr. Bond, and a lady, Mrs. Barber, came forward, and were accommodated with seats on the platform. At this juncture a gentleman in the audience asked if it was necessary that Mr. Evans' slates should be used, as he had brought two with him. Mr. Evans replied that he might bring his slates forward, hold them himself, and see what he could get. He came on the platform, gave his name as Hoskins, and untied the two slates. Mr. Evans examined them to see if there was any writing on them, put a small grain of pencil between them, and returned them to Mr. Hoskins, who tied them up again, and, passing to the corner of the platform, held the tied slates in his hand. Mr. Evans then put new slates, one by one, in a bucket of water standing on the front of the platform, deliberately washed them and dried them with a small cloth before the eyes of the audience and committee, placing a piece of pencil between. Two of them he handed to Mr. Henshaw, a second pair were handed to Mr. Bond, and a third to Mrs. Barber. Another gentleman, named Brown, was invited forward, and supplied with two slates, which were first crossed with a

FAC-SIMILE OF DIRECT SPIRIT WRITING.
Received under Test Conditions at Mr. Fred Evans' Public Seance, Horticultural Hall
Melbourne, Sunday, March 6, 1884.

broad pencil mark by Mr. Evans, and bound together with a strong elastic band. These slates were held up by Mr. Brown before the audience until taken from his hands, and one shown covered with writing, as described later on. Mr. Hoskins stated in answer to a question that he heard something moving between his slates, but he did not know whether it was the pencil. Shortly afterwards he untied the slates, and on one of them was found written the following:

DEAR FRIENDS:—I am pleased to come back and add my evidence to the truth of spirit return. I know many of you do not believe in the possibility of the power of spirits to come back and communicate. But you will all know the grand truth sooner or later.
Your old advocate, JOHN TYERMAN.

—— FRIENDS AND TRUTH SEEKERS:—It is so long since my presence has been made known amongst you that I expect I am almost forgotten. Tell Mr. H. J. Browne (he knows me) that I am glad to see him still upholding the sublime truth of our hereafter. I am overjoyed in having this chance to demonstrate to you that we can come back and give you envitable (?) proof. Yours, ARTHUR DEVLIN.

Mr. Bond's slates were next examined, and one found to be covered with writing; also one of Mrs. Barber's (whose slates had previously been placed at her feet). The pair of slates held by Mr. Brown were then unclosed, and writing in three colors, besides the pencil, found all over them, *written over the lines made on the slates at the time they were closed, and handed to Mr. Brown.*

Mr. Hoskins (the gentleman who had brought, tied, and held his own slates) said he desired to make an important statement to the audience, which was that the two slates had been given to him by Professor Baldwin (who was a friend of his). He thought it only fair, in view of what had occurred, that he should acknowledge this.† Mr. Evans offered to submit the slates to test to prove that the writing on the slates was surface writing, and not produced by chemicals. The slate held by Mr. Brown forms the illustration of the colored slate given herewith. The messages on the other slates were then read as follows:

God bless you my son. I am glad to see you here to-night. We cannot say much of a private nature before an audience like this, therefore we only send you greeting. This from your spirit father. Good-night. JOHN BELL.

The spirit of John Dobson sends love to his daughter. JOHN DOBSON.

MY DEAR* —— ROBERT:—I have come to-night to tell you that though absent in body I am with you in spirit. Your sister, EMILY WEEKS.

The spirit of Mary Foster is here. This from JAMES FOSTER.

Richard Williams is here and sends kind greetings to his son, John--be careful of the market.

DEAR ANN:—I am always glad to write a few lines to you. Tell Alf to be careful of his health. Your father, JOHN FULLER.

†The slates had been marked for identification by Professor Baldwin.
* The writing is effaced by the carelessness of persons putting their fingers on it.

John Bain is here.
My kind love to my sister, from sister in spirit,　　　　　　　EMILY DWIGHT.
MY DEAR SON:—I wish you much joy and happiness.
　　　　　　　　　Your mother,　　　　　　　CATHERINE DEBNEY.
Tell dear mother and father that I am with them to-night.
　　　　　　　　　　　　　　　　　　ADELAIDE M. WILLIAMS.
　Yes, I am here, and am pleased to say that your efforts in that *———— will be successful *————. From your father,　　　　　　RICHARD DWIGHT.
MY SON:—I am with you.　　Your father,　　RICHARD GUILFOYLE.
The spirit of Johanna Stewart *————, also the spirit of Mary Dunbar.
James Lamb and his daughter, Margaret, are here, and send love to Mrs. B *————mb.
My kind wishes to my family and friends. From　　　THOMAS BAMFORD.
The spirits of Mary Ellen Hall and Thomas B. Hall are present, and wish to be kindly remembered to their loved ones. From　　　　　　MARY ELLEN HALL.
MY DEAR WIFE:—My kind love to you. From your husband,
　　　　　　　　　　　　　　　　　　　　　　　JAMES FLETCHER.
James Gill is here.
My love to my children and wife. From your husband,　　WM. P. WALKER.
Also from your father,　　　　　　　　　　　　JOHN DUNBAR.
　MY DEAR DAUGHTER:—I am glad to meet you here, and hope for your happiness in spirit.　　　　　　　　　　　　　　　　　　DAVID WILLIAMS.
Sarah M'Giffin sends love.
DEAR JAMES:—I am joined with mother and father in sending love to you. Your loving sister,　　　　　　　　　　　　　　　　　JANE PORTEOUS.
　　DEAR SISTER:—Your patience will soon be rewarded. Love to all.
　　　　　　　　　　　　　　　　　　　　　　　HARRY CRESWICK.

　FRIENDS OF THE EARTH PLANE:—I have assisted many of your spirit friends to write, therefore you will thus account for the similarity of many of the hand-writings. Many of you, no doubt, wonder why there is so much of the sameness in the tone of these messages—because many of the messages are written by proxy, and private matters are generally excluded in seances of this kind. Besides, each communication must be condensed as much as possible to allow as many spirits as possible to acknowledge their presence. Hoping this will bring many of you to further investigate Spiritualism, I remain your well-wisher. Medium's guide,　　　　　　　　　　　　　　　　　　　　JOHN GRAY.

　MY DEAR BOB:—My best love to you and Laura. My love to the children. Your wife in spirit,　　　　　　　　　　　　　　　　　ANNIE CROOKE.

The following communications were acknowledged by the persons they were addressed to, or friends who knew the communicants, viz.: H. Sellers, M. Bond, R. R. Martin, M. Melville, G. W. Praagst, F. Bond, Richard Russell, ———— Hall, M. Browne, T. Bamford, W. Mary, J. and P. Hall, Jas. Fletcher, W. P. Walker, David Williams, Sarah M'Giffin, J. Porteous, H. Creswick, H. Crook, J. Bell, J. Dobson, ———— Lamb, Maner, A. M. Williams, C. Debney, R. Dwight, M. Foster. The members of the committee testified that the slates were perfectly blank when placed in their hands.

Mr. Terry said it had been announced that Mr. Evans would demonstrate the phenomena of psychography, or direct spirit writing. Though this was

---

* The writing is effaced by the carelessness of persons putting their fingers on it.

more than Mr. Evans had promised, it had been fully accomplished. Not only had writing been obtained on the slates in charge of the committee, but upon slates furnished by Mr. Baldwin, the conjurer and exposer (?) or imitator of spirit phenomena, these slates being retained by the gentleman who had been intrusted with them by Mr. Baldwin during the whole time. In addition to this there were some twenty or thirty persons present who had recognized and identified the communicating spirits. The chairman's remarks and a few words from Mr. Evans to the same effect, were received with applause. Those persons who had received messages were invited to come on the platform to inspect them, and eagerly availed themselves of the opportunity to do so. The slates were subsequently on view at Mr. Bamford's, Little Collins Street.

The whole seance was of a clear and decisive character, and transcended anything of the kind which has occurred here.

We extract from the *Harbinger of Light*, of May, 1889, the following from its well-known editor :

TRANSCENDENTAL PHOTOGRAPHY.

REMARKABLE PHENOMENA THROUGH MR. EVANS.

For six weeks past I have had periodical sittings with Mr. Evans, with the view of obtaining permanent proof of the passage of matter through matter. At the conclusion of the fourth sitting, held on the twelfth of April, I was told by the spirit guide, John Gray, to bring a pair of slates with me the next time. Easter holidays intervening, I did not go up for my fifth sitting till the twenty-sixth, when, being busy till past the usual time, I hurried away with my boxes containing the objects to be acted upon, but forgot the slates. It was not known, either by myself or Mr. Evans, for what purpose these were wanted, but, as I could not go back for them, two new slates were taken from Mr. Evans' stock, and after being wetted and rubbed with a small duster, under my immediate supervision, a piece of slate pencil was put between them, an elastic band round them, and they were laid on the table against the small boxes on which my hands rested. We conversed on various topics (Mr. Evans sitting on the opposite side of the table) for about twenty minutes, the slates not being touched by either of us. At the end of that time Mr. Evans reached across the table, took the band off the slates, and with a look of pleasurable surprise exclaimed, "A spirit photograph." All that appeared visible to me at first glance was a glazed square about 4x5 in the middle of the slate, with writing all round. On holding it to the light, however, three distinct forms were visible. One of them I almost immediately recognized as D. D. Home, the celebrated English medium; the others I did not recognize.

Here was a marvel. Not only had the shadows of these forms been cast by some mysterious process on the interior of the closed slate, but the chemical and varnishing matter had also been introduced and used in a space not exceeding the quarter of an inch, whilst the rims of the slates fitted so close together as to exclude the introduction of a sheet of white paper. The messages around the picture are from four relatives, and one from John Gray, the guide, which reads: "Friend Terry, we have given you this as a test of spirit power." The picture appears to be the work of the artist who generally draws or paints through Mr. Evans, having his signature in the corner, "St. Clair." There are four names written upside down on the top of the picture, one being D. D. Home's, but the others do not appear to belong to the portraits. On the lower slate was the following message:

FRIEND TERRY:—Owing to the peculiar atmospheric changes in your climate, we have found it very difficult to succeed in giving you either the Ring or Leather test. We have first to dissolve the material in order to encircle them together. Twice have we succeeded in accomplishing our end, but at the final the parts, instead of remaining united, have dissolved again into their former state. But if you will have sufficient patience to sit, I am satisfied that we will eventually accomplish those tests.   Your friend,   JOHN GRAY.

Any photographic expert or press representative may see this remarkable production at the office of this paper.   W. H. TERRY.

A SEALED LETTER ANSWERED.

The following is extracted from the *Harbinger of Light*, Melbourne, relative to the experience of one of Melbourne's well-known and respected citizens:

In October last Mr. Creasy sent a sealed letter to Fred Evans containing four questions, to be replied to from the spirit world. The letter was placed between slates by Mr. Evans, and the replies written thereon transcribed to paper and returned to Mr. Creasy, who informs us that the questions were responded to by a friend who passed to spirit world some two years since, but whose name was not mentioned in the letter. Other information is given, to which the letter would give no clue were it either opened or read clairvoyantly by the medium.

DEPARTURE FROM MELBOURNE.

MR. FRED EVANS gave his final seance in Melbourne on the tenth of May, 1889, and on the thirteenth, accompanied by Mrs. Evans and Mrs. T. Harris, left for Sydney by the afternoon express. Quite a number of friends were present to bid them good-bye, and kindly wishes for their welfare were freely expressed.

At the last sitting had by the editor of the *Harbinger of Light* with Mr. Evans (April 9th), twelve signatures of friends and relatives were written on a slate which lay on the table untouched by the medium. These signatures were all different from the hand-writing of the control or Mr. Evans, and five of them bear a very close resemblance to the hand-writings of the persons whom they profess to come from.

An intimate friend of the editor of the above named journal, who is an old colonist and Justice of the Peace, furnished that gentleman with the following particulars of a seance he had with Mr. Evans, where he obtained the following absolute proof of direct spirit writing :

On the twenty-ninth of April he went to Mr. Evans for a sitting, taking with him a pair of book-slates, which he had wrapped up in brown paper and securely tied. Before the seance he told Mr. Evans what the parcel contained, but said he did not think it worth while to open it, as he was satisfied to use Mr. Evans' own slates. He had quite a satisfactory sitting, getting messages from several friends who had passed on. At the conclusion of the seance he took up the parcel containing the slates, remarking that he might as well take them home (his only reason for bringing them being that it was more satisfactory to friends with whom he might be conversing about the phenomena). Mr. Evans told him to stay a minute, and hold the parcel in his right hand. He did so, and in a short time heard writing going on inside. He was about to open the parcel, when Mr. Evans stopped him, telling him that possibly more might be written after he left. On arriving home and opening the parcel our friend found three messages on the slates, signed by three separate relatives.

If any more evidence were wanted to overthrow the "masked slate" theory, the following testimonial from nineteen persons (several of them prominent citizens) who have obtained writing on their own closed slates, would be a clincher.

MELBOURNE, VICTORIA, AUSTRALIA, May 8, 1889.

We, the undersigned, do hereby testify that we and each of us have investigated the phenomenon of independent slate-writing, occuring through the mediumship of Mr. Fred Evans, of San Francisco, Cal., U. S. A., and have obtained writing on the inner surfaces of slates that we and each of us have furnished ourselves, and which were not for a moment permitted to leave our sight.

The messages appearing thereon were always signed by the names of our departed relatives and friends, and information given that we are sure the medium could not have had any previous knowledge of whatever.

Whilst many of us are not Spiritualists, yet we and each of us agree that the messages appearing between our slates were placed there by some invisible intelligent power, independent of the medium.

SIGNATURES.

John Williams, Grain Dealer, Stock Street, Coburg, Victoria.
Edwin Gill, Justice of Peace, Balaclava, Victoria.
James T. Praagst, Government Land Office, E. Melbourne, Victoria.
R. Stewart, Esq., Bourke Street, Melbourne, Victoria.
Charles C. Bell, Esq., 4 Gordon Terrace, Mary Street, St. Kilda, Victoria.
John Carson, Esq., Kew, Victoria.
W. B. Rodier, Justice of Peace, "Rougemont," St. James' Park, Hawthorn.
John Henshaw, Manufacturer, Council Street, Clifton Hill, Victoria.
Thomas Martin, Manufacturer, 122 Rokeby Street, Collingwood, Victoria.
Richard Bond, Builder, Carpenter Street, Middle Brighton, Victoria.
Wm. Overton, Esq.
John Melville, Accountant, 24 Shiel Street, N. Melbourne, Victoria.
William Jackson, Builder, Armadale, Victoria.
E. Sharpe, Illawarra Road, Hawthorn, Victoria.
Daniel Clay, 33 Michael Street, N. Fitzroy, Victoria.
M. Bond, Middle Brighton, Victoria.
William Brown, 47 Napier Street, E. Melbourne, Victoria.
E. L. Melville, Sheil Street, North Melbourne, Victoria.
F. Overton, Melbourne, Victoria.

WHAT A BROTHER OF SENATOR STANFORD SAYS.

The following testimonial from Thomas W. Stanford, of Melbourne, Australia (brother of our Senator Stanford), a careful student, speaks for itself:

MR. FRED EVANS—*Dear Sir:*—As you are about to depart from our shores and return to the land from whence I, too, came, I have thought a few lines from me might be of service to you, as well as a pleasing memento of my personal friendship and appreciation of your straight-forward conduct in this city.

I have much pleasure in stating, and with much emphasis, to whom it may concern (and you are at liberty to use this letter as you please), that I have had several professional "sittings" with you, and that, without asking for special test conditions, you have given me the best possible proof of writing within closed slates without physical contact with yourself.

I would advise those who take an interest in occult force, either in connection with, or apart altogether from Spiritualism, to have one or more "sittings" with you, to note the result carefully, and then put their wits to solve the mystery (?).

Trusting yourself and Mrs. Evans may have a pleasant voyage home, and retain pleasant memories of your visit to Australia, I remain sincerely yours,

THOMAS W. STANFORD.

MELBOURNE, May 11, 1889.

MR. FRED EVANS IN SYDNEY.

FAREWELL ADDRESS TO MR. FRED EVANS.

(Sydney, N. S. W., Australia, September 1, 1889.)

THE following address was presented to Mr. Evans, at a farewell social tendered to him and Mrs. Evans by a committee of his friends and admirers, and held on Wednesday last, at the residence of Mrs. Peryman, L'Avenall, Newtown, Sydney :

To FRED EVANS, Esq., of San Francisco, Cal., U. S. A.

DEAR SIR AND FRIEND:—We, the undersigned, have great pleasure in bearing testimony to your thorough genuineness as a medium for independent slate-writing. We are satisfied that the manifestations of spirit or direct writing witnessed by us through your mediumship were beyond the possibility of fraud or deception. Indeed, words cannot express a too firm conviction on our part in your honesty, integrity and uprightness of character, and this we say in face of the libels of the Brisbane *Telegraph*, and the utterly false and reckless statements of unscrupulous persons respecting yourself. We look upon you, esteemed friend, as a great light in the diffusion of the grand and glorious truths of Spiritualism. That you may long remain in this sphere of existence to perform your noble mission of convincing thousands of the practicability of communion with the so-called dead, is our earnest wish.

We regret that your stay in Sydney will probably not exceed three months, but we trust that at some future time you will make another visit to our city. We assure you that you and your respected lady will carry away, on your departure from Australia, the hearty good wishes of a large circle of friends. With kind regards we beg to subscribe ourselves,

Yours faithfully and fraternally,

‡ James Kingsbury, M. D., Church Street, Newtown.   SYDNEY, N. S. W
* Alfred Edwards, Colonial Architect's Office.   "   "
† Alex. Tucker, Gov. Inspect. of Post and Telegraph Offices.   "   "
   John Victor, Justice of Peace.   "   "
* N. Joubert, Alderman, Hunter's Hill.   "   "
   A. Firth, Secretary North Shore Gas Co.   "   "
* Alfred Gale, Postmaster, Paddington.   "   "

MR. FRED EVANS IN SYDNEY. 183

* E. P. Atwater, M. D., Newtown. SYDNEY, N. S. W.
* A. T. Munro, President N. S. W. Spiritualist Association. " "
* H. Chappel, Real Estate and Mining, 52 Sydney Arcade. " "
* W. H. Murrell, Tea Merchant, 409 Kent Street. " "
* J. H. Smith, Merchant, 302 George Street. " "
* Charles Coghill, Builder and Contractor, Oxford Street. " "
† S. Kingsbury, Church Street, Newtown. " "
  Henry Gale, Post Office, Paddington. " "
  Thomas Peters, Merchant Draper, William Street. " "
* A. Horsepool, 66 Edith Street, Leichardt. " "
* R. M. O'Connell, 8 Lonsdale Terrace, John Street. " "
‡ A. H. Hatfield, Land and Commission Agent, 106 Abercrombie Street. " "
* E. James, 145 Victoria Street. " "
* E. Hansen, Glebe. " "
† F. E. S. Hewison, 93 Morehead Street. " "

Although much debilitated by the climate, and from the accident that befell him at Brisbane, the same success attended him at Sydney as at Melbourne and Brisbane.

Of his success at Sydney the *Harbinger of Light* says:

> Since the cessation of rains and floods at Sydney, Mr. Evans has been fully occupied with sitters, but he complains of the want of sympathy shown by the majority of his so-called Spiritualist visitors, who are more exacting in their demands than some hardened skeptics. Amongst those who have obtained writings on their own slates (mostly tied or screwed together) are the following: Mr. H. Hocking, George Street; Dr. James Kingsbury, John Hodgson, Esq., Mayor of Bowral; Dr. E. Atwater, W. Murrell, W. J. Allen, Esq., Ex. M. L. A.; Mrs. Hyslop, Mr. and Mrs. Fizzell, Mrs. H. Gale, Mrs. James, Mrs. Thompson, Mr. R. Smith, Mr. A. R. Winckler, Mr. Henderson (Richmond River). Mr. H. Copeland, M. L. A., had a pair of board-back slates, made and fastened with a patent combination keyless lock, the method of opening which was only known to himself. Under these circumstances he obtained three messages on his slates.

Mr. Copeland is Member of Parliament for Sydney, N.S.W., and obtained a message from his father, mother, and brother in his own locked slates that he had made to order for the occasion.

* Obtained satisfactory writing upon their own slates.
† Obtained   "   " upon their own corded slates.
‡ Obtained   "   " upon their own screwed slates.

HE CONFOUNDS THE JUGGLERS.

WHILE at Sydney, near the close of his work in the colonies, Mr. Evans returned to Brisbane to confound the juggler, Patterson, and his aiders and abettors. He had intimated his intention of returning there before leaving Australia. The *Telegraph* said he would not. But, like other honorable men, Mr. Evans fulfilled his promise, and proved the *Telegraph's* prediction, like their statements with regard to his psychic gifts, to be false. Following is the account of his success, referred to heretofore, as copied from the *Harbinger of Light:*

He reached Brisbane on the first of August, and the following day announced that on the Sunday evening following he would offer his services free for experiments in psychography, in the Centennial Hall. It was a wet and stormy night, the rain coming down in torrents; nevertheless, an intelligent and representative audience of nearly three hundred attended. Mr. W. Widdop, J. P., presided, and briefly introduced Mr. Evans, who requested the audience to select a committee by vote to conduct the experiments, when the following were chosen:

Mr. P. R. Gordon, Government Inspector of Sheep; Mr. Tolson, Mrs. Judd, Mr. Ranniger, Mrs. Castles. A bucket of water was placed at the front of the platform, and the slates to be used were placed in the bucket in full view of the audience. These were separately washed and dried, the chairman placing a piece of pencil between each pair of them, and handing them to the committee to hold. After holding them for a considerable time, one of the committee said he heard writing going on between his slates—then Mr. Ranniger and Mr. Widdop also heard the same, and, on the slates being opened, twelve messages were found on them, the signatures to the messages being in several instances recognized by persons in the audience.

Mr. Evans then challenged any one to test the writing for chemicals. A simple experiment in this direction was made by washing off part of the writing on one of the slates to see whether it would reappear when dry—as it would if chemically produced—but it did not. At Mr. Evans' suggestion the platform (on which there was no table or screen) was thoroughly examined by the committee and reported free from any paraphernalia, all that was on or about it being the chairs used by the committee, the bucket of water, and eight slates; the slates remained in possession of the committee, and were handed round amongst the audience, who obliterated a considerable portion of the messages in personal experiments. The experiments were highly satisfactory in every particular, and Mr. Evans was frequently applauded. The *Courier* and *Observer* report the proceedings fairly, though they understate the attendance, but the *Telegraph* is silent, which is significant.

Whilst staying at Brisbane Mr. Evans was the guest of Mr. Phippard, contractor, who, being about to remove his family to Sydney, had made arrangements to do so on Tuesday, August 6th. On the afternoon of that day, shortly before the house was vacated, Mr. Evans was surprised to receive a visit from four of the committee who conducted the experiments of the previous Sunday. They informed him that as soon as he left it was the intention of Mr. Patterson to take exception to the conclusiveness of the tests then obtained, on the ground that Mr. Evans had furnished the slates, and requested Mr. Evans to give them a seance there and then, and obtain writing on two slates they had brought with them.

Mr. Evans at first declined, but seeing that their object was a good one he assented, and the whole party retired into an empty room, and the four members of the committee, holding the two slates in their own hands, obtained several messages on them, some of the messages being signed by relatives of the persons holding them. *The room did not contain one particle of furniture, and the slates brought by the committee never left their sight from the time of their arrival till the completion of the messages.*

No more complete test than the above could possibly be given. The Pattersonian *exposé* vanishes before it into thin air; but there is little hope of the truth of the matter being promulgated over the ground where the falsehood has been assiduously spread by Mr. Evans' detractors and the enemies of Spiritualism.

The four members of the committee who obtained this last test were Mr. P. R. Gordon, Government Inspector of Sheep; Mr. J. Tolson; Mrs. Castles, wife of Mr. W. Castles, J. P.; Mrs. Judd, wife of Manager for Scott, Dawson, & Stewart.

Mrs. Castles and Mrs. Judd have each written reports of the seance, from which we glean the following additional particulars, viz.: the slates were purchased expressly for the occasion from Gordon & Gotch's, Queen Street. They were washed, dried, and marked by Mr. Joshua Bailey, J. P., tied together with string, and were in the same condition when the seance commenced. Mrs. Judd, who carried the slates, testifies that they never left her possession from the time of tying up until the parcel was opened, when the seance began.

LETTER FROM JENNY WREN.

THE following account of a farewell social, given to Mr. and Mrs. Evans at Sydney, is from the pen of a gifted lady writer present, whose *nom de plume* is "Jenny Wren," and published in the *Harbinger of Light:*

The joint committees of ladies and gentlemen who tendered the social had decided to express their regard for our friends by making them a handsome presentation.

A beautifully framed illuminated address was therefore presented to Mr. Evans by Dr. James Kingsbury, on behalf of the Spiritualists of Sydney. In reply to this gentleman's able and eloquent address, Mr. Evans (who was looking far from well) replied very feelingly as follows:

"Mr. Chairman, Ladies and Gentlemen:—I thank you most sincerely for these pleasing tokens of your esteem and good-will. Not only will they enable me to carry back to California a pleasing memento of my visit to Sydney, but they will give me the satisfaction of knowing that my work here has been gratefully appreciated by those who have had seances with me, as is proven to-night by these presentations and demonstrations of good feeling towards me.

"While I naturally look forward with pleasure to my return to San Francisco, and the friends whom I know are waiting to welcome me, I feel that I am leaving a sufficient number of good and true friends behind me in Australia to induce me to again visit your colonies at no distant date.

"I am pleased to see many faces here to-night whom I know my advent in Sydney first brought to investigate the claims of Spiritualism; and that they have found sufficient proof to enable them to know that Spiritualism is a mighty truth, is instanced by the hearty manner in which they have worked to bring their social to a successful issue.

"It is not my province to preach spiritual truth from the platform, but rather to demonstrate its phenomena through the influence of my guides; yet I must just here attest its power and beauty to elevate and ennoble all life, and confer the blessing of the knowledge of the continued existence of our loved ones, and the possibility of their communion with us by various means. This truth will surely tend to purify our lives, because no man feeling that those who are so dear to him in spirit-life are watching his actions, reading his motives, and rejoicing in his progress, could wantonly or willfully commit those sins that would grieve these loving friends, and tend to separate him from their gentle influence.

"I will not detain you longer from the pleasures so liberally provided by our hostess, but again express my deep sense of your kind appreciation, and my desire to clasp hands with you again at no distant period."

Amid prolonged applause Mr. Evans took his seat, when Mr. Firth rose, and, in a humorous speech, announced the pleasure he felt in presenting Mrs. Evans, on behalf of the committee, with a handsome gold watch, as a memento of regard from the Spiritualists of Sydney.

The watch was engraved with the monogram, "A. E.," and a neat inscription. Mrs. Evans, who looked truly interesting in her elegant costume, and who seemed almost overcome with emotion, rose to acknowledge the tribute so lovingly tendered by the friends whose respect she had won during her stay in Sydney.

She said, in tones whose quiet dignity impressed me with the deep feeling that caused her to look like a pure white lily receiving the ovation of the flowers, "Dear friends, your kindness to-night almost overcomes me; there are no words in which I can express my sense of appreciation and sincere regard. I always wish that in traveling from place to place I did not attach myself so deeply to those I meet, as this feeling of affection involves the pain of parting, and always causes deep regret. I do not simply form a liking for those I call my friends—I *love* them deeply and truly; and so I feel to-night, as I accept your kind and generous present, that so many more links are formed between my life and yours, and I regret that I must say good-bye. There is in every true woman's heart a sacred place that none but a mother can occupy; next to the husband there is none so dear—no one can fill that vacant place. So that even while I am happy with my husband in his mission, and love all the friends who so kindly extend their sympathy to him, my heart turns fondly toward home and mother. I have no words to tell you how much I appreciate your kindness to both of us, but to thank you very much, and say that I shall ever remember with pleasure my visit to Sydney and the kindness of the friends here. I hope that the desire my husband has expressed may be fulfilled, and that erelong we may be allowed to revisit the Australian colonies, and clasp your hands in greeting."

The social was a pronounced success, the arrangements perfect, and the enjoyment of the evening unalloyed. Dancing was kept up until an early hour, when the guests separated, to meet again on the Wednesday following, on board the "Lobelia," which had been kindly lent by Mr. Joubert for the purpose of enabling the friends to follow the "Alameda" as far as the Heads.

Accordingly we all mustered at the time appointed—three P. M.—and accompanied the tender to the "Alameda." We went on board, inspected the state cabin, social hall, etc., and bade a final farewell to our esteemed friends, Mr. and Mrs. Fred Evans.

Mr. Evans had been very unwell all the preceding week, and looked very pale; but his earnest hand-shake brought tears to our eyes as we realized how truly we had received "visits from angels" through his excellent mediumship, and what a really noble character he possessed. With hearty cheers and God-speed we at last left the fine vessel, Mrs. Evans waving the stars and stripes in response to our handkerchiefs, as far as the eye could follow them. So we parted, and the unanimous prayer of the Spiritualists in the Australian colonies is: "God bless Fred Evans, and bring him and his loving wife safely hither again." JENNY WREN.

It may be in order here to insert a charming little farewell poem, written by the same gifted writer, and which first appeared in the *Harbinger of Light:*

FAREWELL TO MR. AND MRS. FRED EVANS.

Farewell, dear brother-friend; yes, fare-thee-well;
  Love's faithful guardians speed thy way
Home to the "Golden Gate," of which ye tell,
  To the sweet "summer land's" more tranquil day.

Dear friends await thee there in hope to meet thee,
  Fond hands outstretched to give thee loving cheer;
But we who prize thy work, oh! we shall miss thee,
  And hold these sweet mementos very dear.

God speed thee, brother, on thy homeward journey;
  Fair winds and sunny skies be o'er thy head;
Prosperous thy mission still to bless the many
  Who long for tidings from the so-called "dead."

Dear fellow-servant of the truth we cherish,
  Our hearts are all too full to say "good-bye;"

Fond memories of thy love can never perish—
  Immortal as our lives, they ne'er can die.

Be of good cheer; the angel guards around thee
  Will never fail to help and comfort give;
And though the trials of earthly life surround thee,
  Thy Father's blessing sweet relief shall give.

And this thy joy, to comfort human sorrow,
  And bid the mourner dry the hopeless tear,
Since we shall meet again on that glad morrow,
  When every brow the light of love shall wear.

And fare-thee-well, dear sister; we have loved thee
  For all thy gentle kindness, simple grace;
And in our hearts no sweeter memory dwelleth
  Than this fair recollection of thy face.

Go with thy noble husband, and God bless thee;
  Sweet angels teach thee holy truths sublime,
Until in perfect joy love's soul possess thee,
  As beauty's sacred laws thy life entwine.

STRONG ENDORSEMENT.

CHARLES P. COCKS, of Brooklyn, N. Y., writing to the editor of *Harbinger of Light*, has this to say of Mr. Evans' gifts:

I had several sittings with Mr. Evans when I visited California, in the summer of 1888. They were very satisfactory, and the manifestations were most remarkable.

I brought home eight slates and made careful notes of the phenomena which occurred at those sittings; and in taking a retrospective view of the occurrences, with all the additional light and corroborative evidences, the facts remain as astounding as ever.

The tests of identity; the prophecies since fulfilled; the correct answers to my inquiries, together with their marvelous production under test conditions, make up a history of very great interest to me; and although meeting the psychic then for the first time, I have felt ever since a personal interest in his success.

I have investigated the phenomena in most all its phases; and while it is often difficult to draw the line and say which is the most wonderful and important, still I am inclined to think, as was expressed by the late Epes Sargent, that independent writing forms the scientific basis of Spiritualism.

Very respectfully yours, CHARLES P. COCKS.
BROOKLYN, November 28, 1889.

We have a vast amount of matter at our disposal concerning Mr. Evans' work in the colonies and elsewhere, which would only be piling proof upon proof, and might be regarded as tiresome from its cumulative character. The following letter, however, written by H. Mackay, Esq., Surveyor-General of Queensland, Australia, to W. M. Foster, Esq., Sydney Street, Mackay, Queensland, after a sitting with Fred Evans, is too important to omit:

BRISBANE, QUEENSLAND, December 29, 1888.

MY DEAR FOSTER:—I will excuse you for no doubt thinking me dilatory in the matter of dropping you a few lines. * * * I want to say a word or two on a very interesting subject which occurred to-day. I had a sitting with Fred Evans. I talked with Judge Paul at his chambers yesterday and accompanied him down to Evans' place, to whom and his wife he introduced me, and made an appointment for to-day, and the following is what happened:

Evans sat opposite to me at a plain deal table (we were alone in a small, well-lighted room, time twelve midday). From a pile of small slates he took one, thoroughly cleaned it on both sides in my presence, and gave it to me to hold edgewise. After a minute he said it was sufficiently charged with magnetism. He then took another slate, cleaned it, and gave it to me to treat in the same manner. He then dropped upon the first one a few grains of pencil, placed the other slate upon it, gave both into my charge to place my hands upon, which I did, and continued to do the whole time of the sitting.

He next took another slate, going through the same operation of wetting and rubbing both sides clean, dropped a few grains of pencil chips upon the clean surface of the table, and deposited a slate immediately over it. He did the same with yet another, placing it alongside the last one, and then pushed them toward me, and touching the double ones upon which I had my hands. That is all the manipulation he did. We talked on various subjects in an off-hand, chatty manner; suddenly two or three times his eyes appeared to involuntarily close, when he would ask some question about the relationships of some spirit which he could not clearly understand. He told me there were several present, and giving me pencil and a slip of paper, asked me to write some names upon it. I did not expect this because I had some prepared questions in closed envelopes lying on the slates held by me. However, I complied. He turned his head and I wrote merely the *initials* of my mother and two of my brothers, rolled up the paper and held it in my hand. I am quite positive he did not see even the face of the paper upon which I had written. In a few minutes he asked me if I had a brother named William who had passed over, because the spirit standing beside me said he was my brother William, but he could not describe him minutely, owing to want of clearness in the atmosphere—would endeavor to do so directly. He then asked me if I had a wife in the spirit world. I said, "No," upon which he remarked that it was very curious, and appeared unable to understand something. He again asked me (after one of his periods of temporary silence with closed eyes) if I had a departed relative named Elizabeth. Again my reply was "No." After a few minutes of ordinary chat, it appeared to me that a monitory signal was received by him, for he put out his hand and turned over the slates in succession, when, to my intense astonishment, the whole four slates were written upon, one of them quite filled with small writing; in fact, a fairly long letter from my mother, and signed with her name, and the corresponding slate which covered it was about half filled with an affectionate letter from Mary Mackay (whom I don't know at all). Upon another slate was a communication from Evans' guide, John Gray, saying he was glad to have the pleasure of assisting my friends to converse with me and could not do more to-day. And upon the fourth slate was a short letter from my brother William, each line of which was written in a different color—green, pink, blue, yellow—presenting a singular appearance— firmly and clearly written, as, in fact, they all were. Evans gave me the slates to take away, and I intend to preserve them as long as possible.

Now, I have seen what I have long desired, and from henceforth it is impossible for me to maintain the attitude of scientific negation which I have up to the present assumed. Whether it is in our power or within the scope of our knowledge to deal with such matters as this letter relates, I do not know, but this I do know: facts are stubborn things and "Winna ding," and what I have written herein is as positive a fact as can be imagined, and no known material agency can produce a more certain one.

Why should we deny the plain existence of a proved effect on account of our ignorance of the laws which produce it? Well, I am supplied with food for much reflection, and in my next, when I have time to spare, I will revert to the subject, and bring in several things which, until this moment, escaped my memory. I spoke of you to Evans, and he appears to have a high opinion of you. And now, my dear friend, I will say good-night.   *   *   *
Believe me,   Yours very truly,   H. MACKAY.

Mr. Evans returned from Australia covered with honors, bringing with him the highest endorsement of genuineness of his psychic powers from scores of prominent colonists. The Australian climate he found unfavorable to the best results, except by an excessive drain of his vital forces. While in the climate of San Francisco he can readily give from eight to ten seances per day; there, from four to five was all he could endure.

SLATE-WRITING TESTS NOT IN THE DARK.

Medium Evans recently exhibited his powers as a psychographic medium to an *Examiner* man, and did not demand a dark room as one of the necessary conditions. Mediums say the spirits do not work in the dark as much as they did, because they have become better acquainted with the natural laws which govern them.

Evans sat at one side of a small table and the newspaper man at the other, in a brilliantly-lighted room. On the floor near the medium was a pile of small school slates. Evans took one of the slates and exhibited both sides. No writing could be seen on it. He moistened it with saliva and wiped it with a sponge, placed it upon the table, and told the sitter to put his hands on the slate. A few faint raps under the table indicated that the spirit of John Gray was present and getting in his work on the slate. After ten minutes, during which time the sitter had not removed his hand from the slate, the slate was turned over and found to be covered with writing, which was signed by John Gray. Another slate, treated in the same manner, turned up with a recognizable portrait of U. S. Grant and a message signed by the General. Eight slates were used during the seance, and writing was produced upon all of them. None of the messages were written by Evans, whose hands were otherwise employed all the time. Whatever may be the method of producing the messages, it is certain that the slates, after being washed, were not out of the newspaper man's hand for an instant.—*Daily Examiner*, San Francisco.

I ATTEND A SEANCE.

The mysterious thing about the affair is how the medium, Evans, got between the slates to do the writing. At the time the slates were put in my possession I had written no names and had thought of no names. I did not know I was expected to write them. But the truth is that one of the names written by me appeared on a slate, which no one but myself touched between the time I wrote the name on the paper and the times the slates were opened. I do not know how it was done, yet I state but the facts.—*Freethought*, San Francisco.

LETTER FROM CHARLES P. COCKS.

THE following letter from Charles P. Cocks, a prominent citizen of Brooklyn, New York, written to the *Golden Gate*, will be valuable in this connection:

EDITOR OF *Golden Gate:*—The late Epes Sargent, who was esteemed as a writer on spiritual matters, has stated that independent writing and clairvoyance constitute the *scientific basis* of Spiritualism.

There is surely no difficulty in the way of investigating that phase of the phenomena called independent slate-writing, as it can be scientifically demonstrated so as to leave no room for doubt as to the results.

While practically a dark cabinet is afforded the intelligences in which to operate between the closed slates, yet the surroundings are perfectly light for observation. I have noted the following facts in my experiments in the presence of the psychic, viz.:

That the invisible intelligent powers operating can see and hear what any mortal present can see and hear, and, more than that, they are able to answer questions which are written, and not seen by the medium; and even mental questions. The controls tell us that we are not to infer that the spirits are infallible by any means.

If a spirit comes who is a personal friend or relative, he will know us, although we may be strangers to the medium; but if a strange spirit comes, he does not necessarily come in so close rapport as to be able to tell our name, or to read our thought. He must become acquainted very much as mortals would.

I had several most satisfactory sittings with that excellent medium for this phase, Mr. Fred Evans, at San Francisco, in the summer of 1888. I thought this an excellent opportunity to test the phenomena while sojourning in a strange city to me, more than three thousand miles from home.

My first sitting with Mr. Evans was on Monday, July 9, 1888. On my way to his residence I purchased a pair of double slates at a book store, cleaned them, and placed a private mark upon them there. After reaching his residence, I was courteously received by him and invited into the second-story front room for the seance.

We were entire strangers to each other, never having met before. I wanted test conditions as far as possible, so did not mention my name. The room was as light as perfect daylight could make it, and there was no one else present, as mortals, but ourselves. My slates were the first used, and were never out of my sight for a moment. After opening them on the table we placed our hands flat upon them a few moments, to impart magnetism.

Then after placing a small bit of pencil upon one, he closed them and placed them upon the carpeted floor, within three feet of me. Then he placed a small clean slate before me, and asked me to write the names of two or three deceased friends on a slip of paper, to fold it, and place it under the said slate. I did so, writing the name of my father, my wife, and a friend of our family, who passed away more than twenty years ago. These, of course, were not seen by the medium, and were not out of my personal possession. Then we joined hands over the table, he sitting opposite to me. After turning the slate over I found a message signed John Gray (the medium's control), saying substantially that I possessed good powers for obtaining writing if I would only develop them.

Light raps were frequently heard on the table, and Mr. Evans announced that my wife was present. He also announced the name of the friend that I had placed upon the paper, and said she was present, but too weak to communicate as she desired to. He then reached forward and wrote on a slip of paper: "My son, I am here," signing my father's name to it. This was written upside down to him, but right side up to me.

Be it understood, that when I placed the names on the paper under the slate, I made no allusion to relationship, nor annexed any question. While holding my hands over the slate I felt cold currents of air to pass over them.

After he informed me of the presence of my wife, I asked if she could give me her maiden name as a test of identity. (I had not written it on my paper, only the initial.)

Then the medium's hand was controlled to write the name on a slip of paper. The slates were still lying upon the floor, and I asked if she would sign her name in *full* to a message, also to state where she was residing at the time of her decease.

In a few minutes the slates were taken up, and on opening them I found both the inner surfaces full of writing, also a brief message on the under side, toward the carpet, the latter signed with my friend's name.

Those on the interior were one from my father, of a personal nature, addressing me as his son, and signed with his name. The other was a loving message from my wife, addressed, "My dear Charlie," and signed "From the happy spirit of your spirit wife," giving the name in *full* (whereas on my slip I had only written the initial of the middle name as before stated).

Then was added, "Minneapolis is where I passed out," (answering correctly the verbal request I had made).

In this message, among other things, was written: "You will soon receive a good offer for your real estate." This prophecy I will refer to again in the sequel.

The two messages contain 140 words. I brought the slates home with me, together with others, and prize them very highly. The writing is understood to be executed by the psychographic control of the medium, Spirit John Gray, as dictated by the communicating spirits. There is a marked difference, however, in the general style of the writings.

Finally the medium placed a slate on the floor, without pencil, and soon a message was produced on the under side, from John Gray, in green, similar to the prominent shade of color in the carpet.

On the eleventh I had a second sitting. After cleaning a pair of slates in my presence, Mr. Evans placed a bit of pencil between them and a rubber band around them, and threw them upon the floor to await what would come.

I then announced that I would like to ask two or three questions. The medium told me to write them out on paper, which I did; and after placing the paper between two more clean slates, placed them on the floor also. The medium, soon after this, asked me if I had a picture with me. I answered "No." Then he remarked that the control indicated that I had something wrapped in paper. In response to this, I took my wife's wedding ring from my pocket, and removed the wrapper under the edge of the table, out of sight of the medium, but his hand was controlled to write "ring" on the table, and also when the pair of slates first laid upon the floor were opened, both inner surfaces were covered with a single message from my spirit wife, and under her signature was the following: "I am glad you are still carrying my ring."

In the body of the message, which contained 134 words of kind advice and tender affection, it was written: "You will make a sale soon at home," this evidently having reference to the same matter communicated in the first message.

The other pair of slates had the questions, which were placed between them, satisfactorily answered to the point. I should state also that there was another slate placed on the floor at the same time, a single one, making five at one time. This latter, when taken up, was found to be full of writing on the under side, four messages in different styles of chirography, and one in several colors.

At a subsequent sitting, I made the remark that if the spirit of my father, or any of my ancestors were present, I wished that they might be able to tell me what had become of the pedigree which I had either lost or mislaid—it gave my ancestors in a direct line running back over 250 years.

Mr. Evans remarked, "We will see what they say," then cleaned a slate and threw it on the floor. In a few minutes I read, from the under side of this slate, a pertinent answer, signed with my father's name in full, as follows:

> Charles, my boy, when you reach home, I will impress you where to find the written pedigree of your relations. I am pleased to see that you are progressing, and will soon reap the benefits of the present sittings. Good-bye, from father.

The final message that it was my privilege to receive, was obtained while held alone in my own hands. After cleaning two slates thoroughly, and placing a band around them, they were given to me to hold, while the medium kept up ordinary conversation. Presently gentle raps were heard on the table and he asked me to open the slates. The inner surface of one was found covered with beautifully written messages, five in all, and containing 190 words. One of them is so finely written that it needs the aid of a magnifying glass to read it distinctly. These were from the same spirits who manifested before.

And thus ended, very reluctantly, a most interesting and satisfactory series of sittings, for which I shall always feel a deep sense of gratitude to this gifted instrument for his unaffected manner and uniform courtesy. Before closing this narrative, which I fear is already taking up too much valuable space, I wish to refer to the sequel of several of the prophecies contained in these communications.

Although I had asked no leading questions relating to business or property, the message from my wife in the pair of marked slates, which I took to Mr. Evans, contained the prediction as stated: "You will soon receive a good offer for your real estate." After reading what was stated in the next pair of slates from the same spirit that "You will make a sale soon at home," I remarked if it turned out to be true it would be a strong test. The medium said that he had an impression that this property was in Los Angeles. I told him it was not there. Then he was impressed to say, very decidedly, that it was in Los Angeles that I would receive my offer. This was on the eleventh of July. I subsequently visited various places of interest, as the Lick Observatory on Mt. Hamilton, the Yosemite Valley, etc., and reached Los Angeles on August 8th, where I found several letters waiting for me, one enclosing a telegraphic dispatch forwarded from New York and dated July 23d, at a western city where the lots were located, and containing a very liberal offer for them. (I had only just placed them in the hands of an agent on my way to California, and had no idea of being able to sell, that year.)

I therefore telegraphed to my agent to close the bargain, but in due time received a letter saying that the party waited two or three weeks, and not hearing from me purchased other property. I felt disappointed at this, but at once realized the fulfillment of the first prediction.

It was the latter part of September when I arrived home in Brooklyn, and in course of about ten days received a deed from my agent, to execute to another party for the same amount as offered before, and so consummated the sale, and verified the second predictions.

In regard to finding the pedigree, I thought that it would be a useless task to undertake to look for that again, but one day, soon after I reached home, I was arranging some papers in a drawer of my desk in the library, and incidentally seeing some correspondence in one corner, I looked into them, and to my surprise found the written pedigree entire. One or two other matters, highly interesting and important to me, were referred to prophetically by several spirits, and in very decided terms, which have been fulfilled to a remarkable degree.

In conclusion, I have witnessed many phases of spirit phenomena, but I know of none that can prove more satisfactory or convincing to any candid investigator, than this of direct spirit writing.   CHAS. P. COCKS.

BROOKLYN, N. Y., December 23, 1889.

WORDS SPOKEN AT A FUNERAL.

AS all persons interested in psychical research are naturally desirous of knowing as much as possible of the lives and characters of those possessed of these wonderful gifts, we step aside from the main purpose of this volume to speak of the death and burial of Mr. and Mrs. Evans' first born, an infant daughter, aged nearly five months, and also to represent something of the belief of Spiritualists in the state of the dead, as set forth in the words spoken at the funeral by the author:

"Life is but a fitful dream at best, even when full of years, and enriched by the experiences of time. He knoweth best—the Infinite Source of all light and life—whether we live or die. To our human judgment, death should come only to the aged—to the one who has lived his allotted years, and is ready to lay life's burden down, and rest on the bosom of Mother Earth. But the Good Father knoweth best.

"In the light of our beautiful faith—faith that has merged into knowledge—there is no death. This little bud of promise is but transplanted to other bowers, where it will unfold in beauty and loveliness forevermore. Far removed from the temptations and sorrows of earth, we know it will be tenderly guarded and cared for by some loving angel mother, in whose sheltering arms it has already found a home.

"The life beyond is the real life; this, the ever changing and shadowy. There are no sad partings in the homes of the immortals. No sickness comes there to paint the lily upon the cheek of roseate childhood and joyous youth. Pain, suffering, and death belong to the physical body—not to the risen spirit.

"When we lay aside these earthly bodies—when we close our eyes for the last time on earth—and our spirits awaken to the light and glory of the new day, I doubt not we shall all rejoice to realize that we have at last survived the vicissitudes of time and sorrow, and come off victorious over death and the grave.

"This young mother will not need to wait for some far-off resurrection to restore to her arms her lost babe. Its resurrection has already taken place, and no doubt, erelong, it will be manifest to her mediumistic nature. Her eyes will be opened to see, and she will know her own.

"It is the experience of many mothers that their little ones, who have passed on to the other life, are often brought back to them for help and strength. In the silent hours of night, these little angel spirits are brought to the yearning, empty arms from whence they have been taken, where they are lulled to sleep again and again in the bosom of mother love.

"The lesson of this, and all similar bereavements, should be one of abiding trust in the Infinite Spirit of Love, of which all life is a part. He who holds the stars in His keeping, and gives of Himself to every embodied soul, means, in His own good time, the happiness of all.

"There are beautiful homes, and schools, and bowers of transcendent loveliness, in the Summer Land, where the little children are reared and taught; and there are such multitudes of them as no man can number. Mothers, your treasures are all there, safely sheltered in the Father's love, 'where the many mansions be.'

"And so, with these few words, freighted with the heart's deepest sympathy for the stricken parents, we lay away, with tender and tearful care, this little casket from which the jewel has been taken. May He 'who tempers the wind to the shorn lamb,' watch over and guard them by His ministering angels in their journey through life, and bring them at last to the welcoming arms of the matured spirit of their lost darling, who will greet them with outstretched arms on the evergreen shore of immortal life."

SKEPTICISM AND ITS EFFECTS.

MANY persons, even among Spiritualists themselves, are hostile to all physical phenomena. Some even pride themselves on their superior acumen in discovering fraud, from the fact that manifestations that others claim to have witnessed never occur in *their presence*. Wrapped up in the mantle of their own conceit, they do not realize that their superior wisdom is the wisdom of foolishness, and ignorance of the nice conditions and laws governing psychic manifestations. It is no doubt true that, with most psychics, persons with strong magnetic powers can overcome in a measure the power of the spirits to control the conditions. If they cannot overcome the controlling spirit entirely, they can so disturb the sensitive vibrations as to produce jangling inharmony in the quality of the messages. We will illustrate this point with a familiar fact. In Yosemite Valley there is a small body of water known as Mirror Lake. In looking down into the waters of this lake, on a still morning, one will see reflected, as from a mirror, all trees, rocks, and clouds coming within the angle of vision. But cast the most insignificant pebble into the bosom of this lake, and then what do you behold but the jangled and distorted reflections of what before stood forth in the perfection of their reality. Mediumship is alike sensitive to disturbing conditions.

A prominent physician of San Francisco, who is also a member of the California Academy of Sciences, visited Mr. Evans at stated periods for many months, and received long and very interesting messages on a variety of subjects, from a highly unfolded lady spirit. One on the subject under consideration will be found especially to the point:

* * * You put me to much trouble last week in giving you manifestations as your friend suggested. (That is, the sitter carried his own slates, washed and dried them himself, put them down and took them up himself, the medium never for a moment touching the slates or seeing what was written. But I hope you are now free to admit the possibility of direct writing, under conditions which place the slates beyond the medium's control, and that you will not allow any one to influence your belief in spirit writing. * * *

I have been brought to see many mortals who were once happy in the belief that their loved ones came back and communicated with them, and who allowed their skeptical friends to dictate to them and suggest that they should try to force their spirit friends to communicate this way or that way, until they succeeded in breaking all laws of spirit communion, causing their spirit friends to sorrowfully turn away, when they could do no more. And what was accomplished? Nothing—nothing but misery—nothing left but a blank future—all bright hopes dashed to the ground. One of these had allowed his friends to prove that he could stop his spirit friends from communicating. But he could not prove by that they do not exist. Alas! the poor mortal was left to reflect as he might, for he had cut off all avenues of information, and put out the light of his own salvation. You see by this the danger of going too far, and allowing your friends to think for you. Hold fast that which is good, for it will make your stay on earth happy.

The mode of demonstrating through this phase, known as independent slate-writing, is a very sensitive one and very easily spoiled, and would often be were it not for the strong exertions of the medium's spirit guide to overcome all obstacles.

If mortals were only honest in their investigations and would come as little children, expecting the truth, they would get it and would be made happy.

When I say they should come as little children expecting the truth, I do not mean with their eyes closed or with a willingness to be deceived, but with a pure and honest heart, for such a presence encourages spirits from the highest and the holiest spheres of heaven.

Whereas the coming with a distrustful feeling of being cheated conveys that feeling to the medium, and through him it is carried to the spirit world, thereby breaking the circuit of pure magnetism, and causing the spirits to lose confidence in their ability to make known their presence, feeling they will not be received as the loved ones they are, and that their endeavors to identify themselves are met with derision.

Another class of investigators who barricade their own spiritual unfoldment, are those who come to the medium for the first time and propose the strongest conditions they possibly can, to spirits who have never communicated before, and who are as ignorant of the laws of manifestating slate-writing as the most bigoted investigator who insists on his own conditions—conditions which the most experienced spirit communicant often fails to overcome.

For illustration of the ways and means of communicating, I will quote the following: A visits a medium for slate-writing. He has never before had any experience on spiritual subjects, and honestly expresses his ignorance in the matter, and asks the medium to direct him how he shall act to receive some proof that his departed friends still live. He sees two slates washed clean, and is told to hold them in his own hands. His mind is not filled with thoughts of trickery or deception, but with an inward wish that it may be true that his friends can come back. With this receptive flow of thoughts he is unconsciously aiding his spirit friends to manifest for him, and a few minutes later, on being told to open the slates, that he positively knows were clean when given into his possession, he finds them filled with loving and encouraging words, and signed by a hand that he knew when on earth, and he is thus made happy. He comes again and brings his own slates, and they are also filled with kind and loving messages from the spirit world, and he forever remains happy by the knowledge he has gained in this simple yet effective way.

Now comes B. He has already heard of the wonderful doings of these mediums, and laughs at and ridicules the very idea of there being such a thing as spirits; and the idea of their being able to come back and write between slates, rap on the tables, and do other hundred and one things, seems to our clever friend preposterous. The friends he has thus ridiculed prevail on him to go just once to a medium and convince himself. He agrees to go, and determinedly ties, rivets, screws and seals a pair of slates, and then, exultingly holding these slates before his friends, offers to wager with them that no spirit will write between *his* slates.

He now repairs to a medium, with a defiant and insulting air of bravado, making the medium feel uncomfortable, and causing an antagonistic feeling to pervade the room. Is it to be wondered at that this man does not attract any spirit to write for him? No; he has repelled his spirit friends, broken up all the conditions of harmony, placed a strong barrier against every effort his spirit friends might make to prove to him their identity, and the result of the sitting is an entire failure. He now returns to his friends with, "Didn't I tell you the medium couldn't fool me?" He loudly laughs, and tries to make them believe he has "investigated Spiritualism, and found nothing in it."

Alas! how many hours of joy he has missed by his bigotry and opposition. But such are the facts that have come under my notice during my stay in the spirit world.

I hope I have not tired you too much; but these are lessons that all must learn before they are ready to receive much spiritual knowledge. Perhaps my next will be more interesting.

A QUESTION OF PROOF.

THE editor of *Psychic Notes*, published in Brisbane, New South Wales, during the time Mr. Evans visited the colonies, Mr. George Smith, we have found to be a most careful student in the field of the occult. The following, from his pen, is a cogent and analytical argument in favor of the spiritual character of the phenomena of independent writing, witnessed in the presence of Mr. Evans, and others of his class of psychics:

The intelligent investigator looks beyond the exploded theories of fraud and conjuring to explain these phenomena, well knowing that in the light of reason they will not stand. We know that the writing on the slates is not chemically prepared beforehand, because there is no method known to science whereby the marks of slate pencil can be invisibly transferred to the slate and afterwards made visible, so that by the aid of a magnifying glass the dust or minute particles of the slate pencil are distinctly visible on the surface of the slate, thus proving it was written by ordinary slate pencil. We know the writing was not done beforehand by the medium, because in many cases the slates on which the writing appears were not touched by the medium until fastened together and the seance commenced. We know the writing is not done by the hand of the medium, because while the slate rested on our shoulder we have distinctly heard the writing going on between the slates; and we know the writing was done by the pencil placed between the slates, because of the facet worn thereon and the writing being of the same color as the pencil; and the writing taking the form of answers to important questions, and having reference to something suggested after the seance commenced, effectually precludes the possibility of preparation beforehand. Conjurers, by a clever trick, can imitate these phenomena, but they cannot produce like results under like conditions. They will not allow investigators to secure and hold their own slates, nor be in close proximity to themselves; neither are they able to produce certain words or names written down after their preparations for the trick are completed, nor produce the writing in any given color, or in colors when no colored pencils are supplied. Another reason why the writing is not the result of legerdemain is the fact of its oft extremely rapid production, the speed often being at least six times the rate the most rapid penman can write. The average under ordinary circumstances is about thirty words per minute. Psychography exceeds this by far. The editor of this journal received a psychographic message of 296 words on a pair of slates, held in his own hands, which two minutes before presented a perfectly blank surface, and far greater rapidity than this has often been attained.

From the facts we and others have observed, we maintain that the phenomena of psychography occurring here in the presence of Fred Evans have been thoroughly proved, and cannot be summed up better than in the following propositions by that gifted writer, " M. A. (Oxon.)" :

First. That there exists a force which operates through a special type of human organization, and which is conveniently called *psychic force*.

Second. That this force is, in certain cases, demonstrably governed by intelligence.

Third. That this intelligence is, in certain cases, provably not that of the person or persons through whom the force is evolved.

Fourth. That this force, thus governed by an external intelligence, manifests its action in (amongst other methods) the writing of coherent sentences without the intervention of any of the usual methods of writing. Such abnormal writing is conveniently called psychography.

Fifth. That the evidence for the existence of this force, thus governed by external intelligence, rests upon:

(*a*) The evidence of the observers' senses.

(*b*) The fact that a language other than that known to the psychic is frequently used.

(*c*) The fact that the subject matter of the writing is frequently beyond the knowledge of the psychic.

(*d*) The fact that it is demonstrably impossible to produce the results by fraud under conditions similar to those under which the phenomena are obtained.

(*e*) The fact that these special phenomena are produced not only in public, and for gain, but in private, and without the presence of any person outside of the family circle.

Voltaire, in his philosophical dictionary, says: A testimony is sufficient when it rests on—

First. A great number of sensible witnesses, who agree on having seen clearly.

Second. Who are sane bodily and mentally.

Third. Who are impartial and disinterested.

Fourth. Who unanimously agree.
Fifth. Who solemnly certify to the fact.

And if this is so, the phenomena of psychography, as it occurs in the presence of Fred Evans, Wm. Eglinton, Chas. E. Watkins, and numbers of other mediums in the private circle, can be considered proven by the thousands of sensible witnesses who have certified to the fact all over the civilized world. The question now agitating the minds of psychologists is not, Do these phenomena occur? but, What is the cause of them? Many theories are propounded, and many, which failing to square with observed facts, fall short just as they reach the most important points. How often do we hear superficial observers dismiss the subject as mere thought reading. Admitting the possibility of the investigator's thoughts being read by the medium, we still have to face the fact of the writing on the slates, and account for the thoughts getting written down there.

The mesmeric fluid of Mesmer, the "odic force" of Reichenbach, the "nerve aura" of other investigators, are all the one and the same "psychic force," the name given by most psychological writers to the power of force which is supposed to produce these phenomena. Dr. Collyer attributes it to the "unconscious action of the will of the psychic." Dr. Geo. Wylde believes it is produced by the "partially entranced spirit of the psychic, although to all appearance in his normal state at the time;" others, to the astral or double of the psychic, and so we have theories and theories, which go so far until met by some fact they are unable to explain, and then, after all these theorists have had their say, there still remains a numerous, compact, and firm body of observers who believe these phenomena the work of disembodied human spirits. They cogently reason that their hypothesis has the merit of being consistently put forward by the invisible intelligence; and why should this intelligence, when interrogated, invariably return an answer identifying itself with the spirit of some departed human being, if it be indeed, as often alleged, only the liberated spirit, astral, or double of the psychic? This theory is the one that covers by far the most ground; and we must remember, that theory which covers the most of the facts is the most likely to be true. There are, however, many laws of nature we know not of yet to be unraveled; in the meantime, let us go on recording facts until sufficient be accumulated from which a positive deduction can be drawn, and the truth made known to the world.

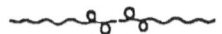

HOW THE WRITING IS DONE.

IN our many and varied experiments in psychography with Mr. Evans, and also with other mediums for the same phase, we have never been able to clearly understand the precise methods employed by the spirits to produce the writing. We say "methods," for we are sure that all do not write in the same way; nor do the same spirits at all times produce the writing exactly alike. And then it is difficult for the mortal mind to understand spiritual things. The conditions on the spirit side of life are vastly different from those of the mortal. We know that the writing is done, but *how* it is done can only, or to a large extent, be a matter of theory and speculation. We know but precious little of spirit chemistry, or spirit magnetism, or how an intelligent will can master the physical conditions necessary to produce the writing. We know that a medium is necessary, a person with a peculiar aura or magnetic force, but wherein this force or aura differs from that of other persons, we are at sea. Not until the scales of mortality shall have fallen from our own eyes, and we see things in that better light, the light of the spirit, shall we be able probably to know much more about it than we do at present. And yet there is really nothing more mysterious in spirit writing than there is in transmitting messages across continents and under oceans on the earth plane. Each is produced in accordance with certain laws, which are as mysterious as the law of growth or of pulsation.

Since writing the foregoing, on the twenty-fourth of December, 1892, we visited Mr. Evans and asked Spirit John Gray to give us, as near as he could do so, an explanation of independent writing as he understood it. He assented, and

Mr. Evans cleaned both sides of six slates and spread them out on the table before us. He then asked John Gray how many more slates he wanted. Eight raps were heard, and eight more slates were immediately cleaned of their dust and bunched upon the floor. In about fifteen minutes three raps announced that the message was written. The fourteen slates were found to be written full, the communication containing about 1200 words. Concerning the diagram produced, John Gray, in a personal note to the author, says, "I could not secure the services of St. Clair to illustrate my chapter, because he is trying to control a relation of his. Therefore, I have made a rude sketch myself, and wish Fred to take the idea to some good engraver and have a design made for the book." This is the longest message ever given by Spirit John Gray at one seance, and we doubt if it has ever been equaled by any other spirit writer. Following is the message complete:

PSYCHOGRAPHY.

Many investigators who have witnessed the phenomenon of psychography (or as it is generally called, independent slate-writing), have repeatedly asked my medium for an explanation as to how the phenomenon is produced. It is for the benefit of these inquirers that I offer the following explanation—that is, as it occurs through this medium:

Many believers imagine that the spirit hand is materialized between the slates, grasps the pencil and proceeds to write. Others believe that in every case where the signature of some friend or relative is attached to a message, that the message is written by the spirit personally, and this is generally the cause of much controversy and skepticism. For instance, Mr. ———— visits the medium perhaps for the first time. He obtains several messages with the names of his spirit friends attached. The wonderful manner in which the message appears takes him by surprise, and he takes the slates containing the messages home. Then comes the careful, critical examination of the messages. Perhaps his wife or some friend suggests that the hand-writing is not "John's," and this fact brings on doubts; then in another message they discover that some letter is misused in the spelling of the name, etc., and so it goes. This is because the investigators are ignorant of the laws governing the phenomenon. Now, let me offer a solution to this seeming defect:

In the first place, we cannot expect spirits, who are ignorant of the law governing the transmission of messages by psychography, to be able to send a message until they have been properly instructed how to do so. Would it be reasonable to ask some of you mortals, who have never studied the art of telegraphy or typewriting, to immediately send a message by these methods? No; they must be given time to learn, and in the meantime if they wish to send a message it must be done by proxy. So it is in the spirit world. All laws must be studied, and until they have educated themselves, spirits must depend on the aid and tuition of other spirits who have become familiar with this mode of corresponding. So you see, many times I and other spirits are called upon to write messages for spirits who do not understand how, and we may spell their names wrong and make other errors, because we take their names phonetically; besides, the message would appear more stereotyped than if written individually by the spirits who desire the messages sent. But this is only for a brief period, for all spirits can learn to write themselves, and when they do so (which they have done hundreds of times through this medium), investigators will receive a *fac simile* of the hand-writing their spirit friends executed when on earth, besides a personality in their messages that will satisfy them as to their identity.

Now, the writing is not produced either by personal contact of the medium or his spirit friends. Everything done in the spirit world is governed by a natural law, and it would be an unnatural law that would permit a materialized hand to go between the surfaces of slates one-sixteenth of an inch apart and grasp a pencil with which to write. The principal methods that we use to transmit messages are by a law that is beginning to be well known and understood by you mortals on earth, viz.: electricity and magnetism. Psychography is produced exactly as telegraphic messages are produced. Let me explain: Suppose A, in New York, wishes to send a message by telegraphy to B, in San Francisco, is it necessary for him to come to San Francisco to do so? Certainly not; he merely operates on his key in New York, and every letter or sound is reproduced in San Francisco. Suppose I wish to send a message by psychography. I write on slate A (see diagram) in the spirit world. The medium being a sensitive, I establish a circuit or current, C, (we need no wires to conduct the current, and in the near future you mortals will learn to dispense with them) to and through the medium D to your mundane slate B, so that every movement made by us on the spirit slate is responded to by the pencil on the mundane slate, and is reproduced. So you see we use the medium for a battery, and your earth plane for a ground, to establish our circuit.

We also have other methods of producing the writing, etc. One of them is by transference, that is to say that we can prepare sufficient writing or

pictures in the spirit world to fill the surface of the medium's slate, and then transfer it instantaneously upon said slate (one example of this kind was produced through this medium in the presence of Professor A. R. Wallace). To produce this manifestation we must first thoroughly sensitize the slate to be operated upon, and disentegrate the pencil into fine powder and precipitate it evenly over the surface of the slate. The transfer is made somewhat similar to photography. The color writing is produced through somewhat the same method, except that the color matter is procured on your earth plane and brought into the room and on the slates in almost invisible dust or powder, and precipitated on the slates the same as the former. These latter methods are much more difficult to produce, and better conditions are required. It is also indispensable to have the medium in a healthy state, free from all mundane worry and annoyance, with pleasant surroundings, and everything that is possible to make him happy, harmonious, and contented. This is important, and good mediums for this phase should not be overworked, but should be carefully protected by those who value the evidence obtained through their mediumship.

As a parting word to investigators, I would recommend that they approach the medium for investigation in a pleasant, harmonious manner, *with their eyes wide open* if in doubt, and they will win the medium's sympathy, and thus make conditions which will insure good results instead of as is the case with many who, with loud voices, while admitting they have never sat with the medium, proclaim their belief that the manifestation they expect to receive *will* be all fraudulent. I suppose it is human nature for all to rebel at insults and aspersions against their honesty, and especially is it the case when the attack is made by parties who admit that you have never given them cause for these cruel charges. A medium being more sensitive than the ordinary run of mortals, feels these insults more than they, and the result is that the possibility of a satisfactory seance is spoiled by the rebellious state of the medium. Yours in aid to a knowledge of a future life,

John Gray.

CONCLUSION.

IN the preparation of this volume we could readily have filled its pages with personal experiences of the author with the psychic, Fred P. Evans; but that, of course, would not have been well. Hence, the large array of experiences of other investigators we have garnered here—of people, many of whom are eminent in science, letters, or in social and public life. Neither have we thought it best to tell their interesting stories in our own language, but often in the language of skeptics, or of persons against whom the charge of friendly prejudice in their favor could not reasonably be made. And thus does this book commend itself to all thoughtful investigators in the realm of psychic phenomena.

No true scientist can afford to place himself in an attitude of hostility towards any fact of nature. He should hold his mind open to proof, and not allow his prejudices to prevent his giving to all proper evidence due weight. What right has any one to conclude that he has exhausted the knowable in the matter of natural law, or of any of the forces of nature? What should we think of the judge who should pass in judgment upon a case, before the testimony as to the facts was all presented and properly weighed? The true scientist is passive and receptive, and slow to condemn what he does not thoroughly and fully understand.

What is there in these phenomena, that have been herein so abundantly testified to and most conclusively proven, that skepticism should sneer at, or science repel? They show that outside the realm of the material universe, as apparent to the physical senses, there is a universe unexplored, of spiritual realities, real and tangible to the spiritual sense—a sense latent with most people, but partially developed with many, and occasionally so complete and rounded out in a few organisms as to bring the mortal in close touch and sympathy with the denizens of that world, who are no other than the children of earth who have passed from mortal sight.

The materialist can see nothing more for man beyond the confines of this life; but the narrowness of his vision is no argument against man's continued existence. The independent writing we have so fully demonstrated in this volume is but one of the many avenues of communication between the living and the so-called dead. It cannot be explained on any other theory. Unconscious cerebration cannot place intelligent messages within closed slates. There is no individuality or personality in nothing. There must be a something that does this writing, and that something invariably declares itself to be the spirit of some departed mortal. Why should we not take it at its word? It is the only rational solution of the question.

The trouble with the materialist is that he has not learned to draw the line between matter and spirit. In all of his estimates and calculations he stops too soon. He gauges the limit of the material universe by his capacity to comprehend it. Like one afflicted with nearsightedness, he cannot realize that beyond the range of his obstructed vision there may be beautiful valleys, grand mountains, and delightful vistas apparent to other eyes. And then scientists are apt to be slaves to their own conceits, if not to public opinion, like Huxley, Carpenter, and the Harvard professors, or the professors of the Pennsylvania University, whom Honorable A. B. Richmond so pungently criticised and reviewed. They do not like to be considered odd or cranky—that is, some of them do not. Professor Crookes was not of this class, nor Wallace, nor Varley. The German scientists, Zöllner and Hollenbach, were brave and outspoken, in the face of a vast amount of educated prejudice. So was our own Professor Hare, and those noble luminaries of the bench and bar, Judge Edmonds, and A. B. Richmond.

Some of our religious teachers, strange as it may seem, have taken very unkindly to our facts. They insist upon our believing through faith what they are unwilling to accept upon proof. They think we should take the story of the appearance of Moses and Elias at the transfiguration of Jesus as a fact, and reject the idea that the spirit of Katy King appeared to Professor Crookes. They hold to the appearance of Jesus to his disciples, in an upper room in Jerusalem, after his crucifixion, but regard the psychography of Fred Evans, Dr. Slade, and others, as the tricks of jugglery. They are not to be censured for this. Men are not to be expected to change all their modes of thought in a day. The theology the child is taught to believe in his infancy, as taught in his catechism—a creed that has become inbred in his nature, cannot be uprooted in a moment. These criticisms do not apply to the Roman Catholic Church, which church has always taught communion with the spirits of the departed; not, perhaps, in the way practiced by what is known as physical mediums, but by visions, inspirations, impressions, etc. The "communion of saints" is also a fundamental doctrine of the Episcopal Church, but never, we believe, in ways as practiced by Spiritualists and psychics.

Psychic gifts are found to be wholly independent of mental or moral qualities. One may be a good musician or mathematician, and yet be wanting in qualities of moral excellence. So with what is known as mediumship. It is this fact that has led many good people to distrust the genuineness of psychic gifts. Our psychics sometimes do things not in accord with the teachings of the spirits. So do other spiritual teachers. We should be as reasonable and charitable toward an erring psychic as we are, or should be, toward other weak and erring mortals.

Less than half a century has transpired since the rappings were first heard in the Fox family, at Hydesville, New York. Since then the strange phenomena have swept over all lands. There are now, no doubt, more believers in the genuineness of these phenomena upon the globe, than there are of any one of the religious sects, not excepting the Catholics, and the cause is spreading as never before.

The world need not deplore its extension. True religion has nothing to fear from this innovation of modern thought. The invisibles invariably teach purity of life and conduct. They tell us, without exception, that if we would win happiness in the other life, we should practice good deeds here—that we should be kind to each other, charitable to the poor, and good to all. They ever urge upon us the necessity of right living here, as the only way to secure those spiritual rewards that will be ours in the sweet Summer Land of the Soul, that lies just beyond the gates of time. They tell us that the consequences of wrongful acts here will follow us into the Beyond, where they will shadow and sadden our spirits until the wrongs of our earthly lives are purged away, and our spirits placed upon the shining way with faces turned toward the delectable mountain of Eternal Truth.

And here we patiently wait for further developments, which, in the coming years, will bring all thoughtful minds to a realization of the mighty fact that

"There is no death, what seems so is transition,"

to other planes of life, growth, thought and action.

Finis.

www.ingramcontent.com/pod-product-compliance
Lightning Source LLC
Chambersburg PA
CBHW020825230426
43666CB00007B/1107